Praise for *You're Never Weird on the Internet (Almost)*

"It's hard to keep up with Felicia Day. She's an actress, a gamer, a screenwriter, a songwriter, a producer, a director, a webmaster, a costumer, and queen of the geek girls. It's hard to imagine where such a prodigy could have come from. Wonder no longer. Felicia tells all . . . well, most . . . well, some . . . in her new book. Reading this is like sitting down and having dinner with her, and hearing the story of her life between the clam chowder and the cheese-cake. I can't imagine a more charming or amusing dinner companion. Felicia is a lot of fun, and so is her book."
—George R. R. Martin

"I came for the delightful snark, I stayed for the disarming frankness and the hard-won insights about the internet—Felicia Day uses the internet to distribute entertainment, but she understands that it's really there to be the nervous system of the twenty-first century."
—Cory Doctorow, coeditor of Boing Boing
and author of *Little Brother*

"Math nerd defies physics! Felicia Day, who is woven from moonbeams, has written a book that seems lighter than air but that ends up punching you firmly in the emotions. Felicia lays out a hilarious tale of how her unique upbringing, eclectic skill set, and killer work ethic led to *The Guild*, one of the pioneering works of online creativity. In the process, she pulls you inside her delicate skull, so that the final moving chapters aren't as much read as they are experienced. An excellent book."
—Jane Espenson, writer for *Buffy the Vampire Slayer*,
Once Upon a Time, and *Husbands*

"Felicia Day gives us an achingly funny, honest, open look at being 'situationally famous' (I love that phrase), plus the vital art of finding your creative joy, and weathering the storms that follow. It's a wonderful book. Buy it before I grab all the copies."
—Rachel Caine, *New York Times* bestselling author
of The Morganville Vampires series

YOU'RE NEVER WEIRD ON THE INTERNET (almost)

[A MEMOIR]

FELICIA DAY

FOREWORD BY JOSS WHEDON

Touchstone

New York London Toronto Sydney New Delhi

Touchstone
An Imprint of Simon & Schuster, Inc.
1230 Avenue of the Americas
New York, NY 10020

First Touchstone hardcover edition August 2015

TOUCHSTONE and colophon are registered trademarks of Simon & Schuster, Inc.

For information about special discounts for bulk purchases,
please contact Simon & Schuster Special Sales at
1-866-506-1949 or business@simonandschuster.com.

The Simon & Schuster Speakers Bureau can bring authors to your
live event. For more information or to book an event contact the
Simon & Schuster Speakers Bureau at 1-866-248-3049 or
visit our website at www.simonspeakers.com.

Interior design by Jill Putorti

Photo credits: Shutterstock: 12, 15, 21, 53 (© Ronen Boidek), 150, 167; David LaPorte:
90; Ron Jaffe: 103; the Bui Brothers: 147, 187 (*bottom left*); Christopher Cruz: 196;
Forrest Huff: 205; Christina Gandolfo: 228. All other photos courtesy of the author.

Manufactured in the United States of America

10   9   8   7   6   5   4   3   2   1

Library of Congress Cataloging-in-Publication data is available.

ISBN 978-1-4767-8565-3
ISBN 978-1-4767-8567-7 (ebook)

For my mom, who is kooky and unique and taught me to be both those things and more. Even though my childhood wasn't "normal," she did her best to help me become who I am, and I love her for it.

Contents

Foreword

by Joss Whedon

There's about twelve guys in very fine suits, scratching their heads. I'm in a boardroom at a major Hollywood talent agency, having just presented my internet musical, *Dr. Horrible's Sing-Along Blog*. With me are the other writers: my brother Jed, my sister-in-law Maurissa, my brother Zack, and Felicia Day. Though we've created the piece, we have no clearer idea of what to do with it, how to actually put it on the internet, than these fine-suited minds do. They hem and we haw. Their resident internet expert suggests tentatively that we could maybe put it on YouTube—but only if we cut it up into three-minute bits, because no one watches more than three minutes of anything.

Which is when the redhead pipes up.

I've asked Felicia to come because I know she's internet savvy; her series, *The Guild*, was a guidepost for me in mounting *Dr. Horrible*. I've sat with her, a couple of times, to learn about how it all works. I know she knows her stuff, but it's still a surprise and a delight to hear her take the conversation and just run with it, own it, slam-dunk it, knock it out of the park—. She sports-metaphors the **shit** out of that meeting. Talks rings around all of us, experts included: *This site has the bandwidth but not the views; this one requires a fee; yes we could go here and charge up front but we'd be compromising the ethos of the endeavor. . . .* I'm practically glowing, watching this girl, who looks all of fourteen, school a roomful of Professional Agent-Men and I realize, oh, of course: I'm having a *Buffy* moment. They never saw her coming.

I have personal heroes, and Felicia Day is one of them. She's kind and loyal and funny and weird—but that describes a lot of my friends.

She's pretty and I want to touch her hair—but that describes, sadly, almost *all* of my friends, including the lads. But Felicia has something few of us do. She's fierce. She's more than a self-made woman—I sometimes think she's *not* a human woman, that she willed herself into existence, before willing the world to make a place for this new, unfathomable creation. Felicia is stronger than I am, and stranger than I am, and she double-majored in math and violin (which she felt compelled to tell me within five minutes of meeting me). I love her for all these things. I love this book because it relates, hilariously and occasionally harrowingly, how she came—or brought herself—to *be* this singular (though double-majored) creature.

It's hard being weird. No—it's hard living in a culture that makes it hard. This book deals with hard—without rancor, without the ugly flush of one-upmanship. Felicia created a persona of the bewildered waif who somehow manages to manage (and occasionally triumph). That persona is a gloss on a similar, but more painful, reality. Her odd, compelling journey was more difficult than a lot of us who knew her knew. But that's part of her gift: she makes crippling anxiety look easy.

Another part of her gift is that she's damn funny. Even if she'd come from the heart of normcore, her tale would be worth telling and well told. But she was raised in Crazytown, and the more foreign her territory, the more delightful—and somehow more relatable—her tale becomes. Reading this book is like spending an afternoon with Felicia, hearing breathless tales (they're always breathless—Felicia doesn't pause when she talks) of achievement, despair, and dazzling, almost transcendent nerdiness. This is the story of someone who found her place in a corner of the world that *literally* didn't exist till just before she showed up. Felicia's place is always off the edge of the map, where dragons wait, and this story is more than a memoir. It's a quest. If you wanna survive, stay close to the redhead.

She knows her way.

Introduction

Whereby I introduce myself to people who have no idea who the hell I am, but have found themselves in possession of this book. Welcome, stranger!

I recently experienced the perfect summary of my career at a Build-A-Bear store inside a suburban mall in Lancaster, California.

Okay, sure, a single adult woman in her thirties with no children might not necessarily pick that as the *first* place to kill an hour of her life. But I'd never been inside one before, and I'd already spent twenty minutes outside like a creepster, watching actual legitimate customers (mostly toddlers) go inside and, like modern-day demigods, craft the companion of their dreams. At a certain point, after eating two Auntie Anne's pretzels, I decided to throw off the societal yoke of judgment.

Get in there, Felicia! Build yourself a stuffed friend. No one's around to witness your weakness!

So I entered, told the saleswoman I was browsing for "a nephew," and proceeded to spend forty-five minutes trying to decide what design to get. My mom wasn't there, so I could take as long as I wanted. Unfortunately.

There was a six-legged octopus that almost took my heart, but after much agonizing, I settled on a stuffed Santa Claus. Because it was July, and a stuffed old man doll seemed more ironic. (The hipster attitude helped get me over the shame that I was buying a *STUFFED ANIMAL FOR MYSELF.*)

I moved on to the accessories aisle to dress my Santa. And proceeded to have a small panic attack. Because my impulse was to dress him in a flouncy pink tutu, but it was a small town and I didn't know if it would offend the saleswoman to make Santa a cross-dresser. But then I thought a liberal stance on the issue might, in a small way, help promote transgender rights in the area . . . when I turned to see four hip girls standing at the end of the aisle. Staring at me.

Eagerly.

I overcame my social anxiety about people I don't know turning their faces toward me and waved. "Heyo!"

They waved back simultaneously, standing in a clump together, four feet away. Practically a gang. (Not really.)

"Hi!" "Are you . . . ?" "You're her, right?" "Hey!" They seemed excited.

I wanted to smile back but stopped myself. I had to check something first. "Uh, who do you think I am exactly?"

"You're Felicia Day, right?"

"Yes! That's me! Nice to meet you!" I always double-check where people think they know me from, because one time at San Diego Comic-Con, a guy bought four DVDs of my web show from me, and as I ran his credit card, he said, "My wife is going to love this gift. You're her favorite actress. She adored you in *The Devil Wears Prada*!"

Doh.

The girls crowded toward me. "We work at Hot Topic next door!

Steph recognized you when you were standing outside at the benches FOREVER."

So much for anonymity at the Lancaster Build-A-Bear.

"Uh, yeah! I couldn't decide if I wanted to come in here or not. Most people my age don't buy things here for themselves, right?" I laughed awkwardly, waiting for them to reassure me.

"Yeah, it's mostly for little kids."

Moving on. "Nice to meet all of you. Did you guys want to take a picture or something?" They were brandishing their cell phones like an extremely amiable group of paparazzi.

"Yes!" "Sure!" "Thanks!" All four of them clustered around me, trying to get simultaneous selfies, like a six-armed octopus of their own, as a mother and child approached.

"I can take those pictures for you." The mother gathered all the phones as she stared at me. "Are you an actress?"

"Uh, kinda. And a producer and writer. More of that lately, to be honest." She stared at me blankly. "Yes, I'm an actress."

"Are you in the movies?"

"Nope. No movies." I wanted to make it abundantly clear to everyone in the Lancaster mall area that I was NOT Emily Blunt.

One of the Hot Topic chicks piped up. "She does tons of internet stuff!"

"And TV!"

One of them leaned in slightly too close. "I love you on *Supernatural*."

She smelled like cherry ChapStick. I liked it. "Thank you."

The mother was confused.

"Is that a TV show? I don't watch it. But I love *Law & Order:*

SVU." The woman called over to her eight-year-old. "Jenna, baby, do you recognize this lady?"

The kid stopped poking through a collection of pastel princess outfits to look me up and down in a surly way.

"Nope."

I opened my mouth to lecture the kid on how princess dresses reinforce sexual stereotypes when the Build-A-Bear saleswoman walked up to join the crowd.

"How's it going back here?"

One of the Hot Topic girls spoke up. "We're just grabbing a picture with Felicia Day! She's awesome." I thought to myself, *I should bring these girls with me everywhere.*

"Oh. Are you a celebrity?"

"I didn't recognize her either!" said the mother. She smiled at the saleswoman in camaraderie, which was kind of crappy but understandable. I'd have the same reaction if I encountered a reality star I didn't recognize. Or a sports person. Or a lot of other internet stars, really.

One of the Hot Topics, the ChapStick one, came to my defense. "It's Felicia Day! She makes tons of videos online."

"Internet videos? Do you do pranks or something?" said the saleswoman.

Oh, hell no. "No pranks, no kittens, no extreme sports, or music parodies. Probably why you don't recognize me, ha!"

"Probably."

One of the other Hot Topics said, "I only know you because my boyfriend is into your gaming stuff. He has a huge crush on you." Then she gave a reassuring smile. "I'm cool with it!"

"Great, that's a real compliment!"

I hear this a lot. The insecure part of me always feels like there's a backhanded insult underneath, like the girls know I'm not QUITE hot enough for their guy to go through with a hookup. Sometimes I think to myself, *I can steal your boyfriend. WORRY ABOUT ME!*

At this point, I realized that I needed to move the conversation along.

"I think we can just take the pictures now and go about our bear building . . ." The mother was already ahead of me and snapped the first iPhone photo as I was midsentence.

I tried to freeze retroactively into a rictus smile, one I've perfected over the years to prevent me from looking like I have palsy in the thousands of pictures that are tagged on Facebook, but I had a feeling it was too late. I leaned forward, "Can you just take that one again . . . never mind." She had already moved on to the next phone. It was fine; people have palsy. I could look like I have palsy, too.

As we took the photos, the saleswoman texted on her phone, then called over.

"Hey, I just texted my son, and he's never heard about you. And he's online all the time."

"It's a big internet . . ."

"He's on there a LOT."

"Uh, I'm sorry?"

One of the Hot Topics started going Team Felicia on her. "He's probably one of those online trolls who hate on women."

"My son is very respectful of women, thank you."

"You never know . . ."

I could smell the situation going south. "We don't need to get in a tussle, guys. Everyone on the internet is a jerk sometimes, ha!"

Hot Topic drew back like I'd slapped her. "I'm not!"

Leave it to me to alienate my own roadies. "Oh, I didn't mean . . ."

The mother taking photos broke in and shoved her kid toward me. "Jenna, get in there and take a picture!"

"But I don't KNOW her, Mom!" We posed, the kid's body language *screaming* of apathy, as a beefy military-type guy came strolling up to the saleswoman with a pair of Teenage Mutant Ninja Turtle dolls in hand. "Ma'am, can you show me where the nunchakus are?" He looked over at my doll and scowled. "Is that Santa Claus in a tutu?"

Annnnd . . . that was my cue to head for the exit.

"It was nice to meet everyone!" I grabbed literally anything nearby to accessorize my stuffed Santa—because he was *not* leaving Lancaster naked—and backed away toward the cash register, waving like an idiot on a parade float. "You guys rock, thanks for supporting my work!"

Two hundred dollars' worth of plastic skates, sunglasses, and mini-electric guitars later, I left the mall. This is what I built, if you're curious:

Yes, Santa's holding a light saber.

Then I drove to where I was headed before I stopped at the mall: to meet Richard Branson.

(Okay, I had to type it that way because it sounds impressive. I was technically not meeting him *personally*. I was touring his Virgin Galactic spaceship hangar on a social media PR invite. But during the event, I stood two feet away from him on up to <u>four</u> occasions, and he was wearing a hot leather jacket and had perfectly coiffed hair. Definitely smiled in my direction. So yeah, we're besties.)

All in all, it was a completely typical day in my life.

Not.

Based on that story, I don't think it's unreasonable to make a stab-in-the-dark assumption: You're either extremely excited to read this book (inner dialogue: "OMG, FELICIA DAY WROTE A BOOK!"). Or extremely confused (inner dialogue: "Who is this chick again?").

For the excited: Thanks for liking my work! I like you, too!

For the confused? I hear you, man. The friend who gave you this book does not know you *at all*. They should have gone with a more impersonal choice, like a scented candle or a gift certificate to somewhere with good french fries, amiright?

But do I at least look a *little* familiar? Like the girlfriend of one of your cousins? I've been told I have a significant-other-of-a-distant-relative quality to my face.

Or just a little bit of Emily Blunt in the eyes area?

I'm not begging, I'm just asking.

Forget it.

I know I shouldn't introduce my own memoir with this amount of insecurity, but my personal life philosophy is always to assume the worst, then you're never disappointed. ← BAM! Highlight that previous sentence, baby! It'll be one of *many* quotable life-nuggets you'll be able to pull from this thing. I'm SUPER good at inventing Hallmark-type solipsisms. Later in life, I plan on making my fortune with a T-shirt/mouse pad/coffee mug company. I'll call it Have a Nice Day Corp.! because of my last name, har har!

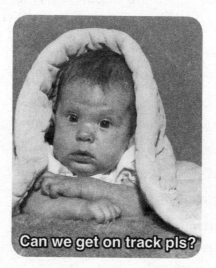

Can we get on track pls?

Yes. Sorry.

Hi, I'm Felicia Day. I'm an actor. That quirky chick in that one science fiction show? You know the one I'm talking about. I'm never on the actual poster, but I always have a few good scenes that make people laugh. As a redhead, I'm a sixth-lead specialist, and I practically invented the whole "cute but offbeat hacker girl" trope on television. (Sorry. When I started doing it, it was fresh. I promise.)

I'm the writer, producer, and actress/host/personality of hundreds of internet videos. Literally hundreds. I have a problem, guys (let's talk more about it later). A lot of people know my work. And a lot of people do not. I like to refer to myself as "situationally recognizable." It's way better than "internet famous," which makes me feel like I'm in the same category as a mentally challenged cat or a kid doing yo-yo tricks while riding a pogo stick. I know that kid, super talented. But the cat . . . not so much.

Seven years ago, I started shooting internet videos in my garage with a borrowed camera, and now I juggle acting on television with writing, producing, and running a web video production company called Geek & Sundry. I'm a social media "aficionado" (née "addict"), I have well over two million Twitter followers, and I'm usually the lone female on lists of prominent nerds, lauded as the media-anointed "Queen of the Geeks." It's a title I reject personally, but when someone else uses it, I go ahead and enjoy it as a compliment. Because who *doesn't* want to inherit a dynasty just because of their gene-stuffs? No work, just <SPLAT>! Born special!

On average, a random person on the street won't know my work, but there are certain places where I'm a superstar, like San Diego Comic-Con, and . . . other places like San Diego Comic-Con. Oh, and I have a HUGE barista recognition factor. Seventy-five percent of the time when I'm ordering my "almond milk matcha latte with no sugar added, lukewarm, please," I'll be recognized by an employee. And yes, my order is a pain in the ass, but I'm determined to enjoy the liquid indulgences of modern life. Might as well take advantage of it all before the zombie apocalypse. I have no practical skills; I'm fully aware that I'll be one of the first ones "turned." Instead of learning motorcycle repair or something else disaster-scenario useful, I'll order the drink I want until I become a shambling corpse.

And I won't be defensive about it, okay?!

I'm very grateful for the weird niche I've created in life. Some people know me *only* from my Twitter feed. That's fine, too, because I, objectively, give VERY good tweet.

Felicia Day @feliciaday · Mar 28
Sometimes I wanna buy a shirt made for a baby and try to get it on, just to be able to think, "Wow, I'm larger now than I was before."
↩ ⇄ 265 ★ 855 🔖 ⋯
Wacky

Profound ⟶
Felicia Day @feliciaday · Mar 12
I have an inner me that's sometimes kind of an asshole to myself.

Felicia Day @feliciaday · Mar 29
Just saw someone leaning into their car trunk and said, out loud to myself, "Dat Ass." Internet, what you done to me? :(
↩ ⇄ 548 ★ 1.7K 🔖 ⋯
Tech Relevant

RELATABLE!!!
Felicia Day ✓ @feliciaday
23 Sep 10 🐦
Learned a lesson AGAIN tonight: Check the menu before entering or you'll get trapped after they serve water and you'll pay $24 for ravioli.

Frankly, I'd hate a life where everyone knew me and people made money selling pictures of me without makeup to tabloids. I'm not in the business of wearing makeup every day. Or going out of my house on a regular basis. I'm most comfortable behind a keyboard and . . . that's it. Real life is awkward for me, like wearing a pair of hot shorts. There's no way to walk around in those and NOT assume people are snickering behind my back about droopy under-cleavage.

The informality of the online world makes it feel like I'm less a "celebrity" and more a big sister my fans can be brutally honest with. "Felicia! Loved your last video. You looked tired, though; take melatonin, it'll help with the jet lag!" They know me as a sort of digital friend, not an object to be torn down over superficials. (Probably because I don't give them much "objectifying" material.)

The best part about this weirdly cobbled-together career I've built is that

I get to bury myself in all the subjects I love. Comics, video games, DVDs, romance novels, TV shows, bad kung fu movies. It's all *part of my job* to purchase these things and mostly legally deduct them from my taxes. And it makes it easier to connect with people, no matter where I am in the world. When the occasional stranger approaches me at a party to say, "Hey, you're Felicia Day. Let's talk about that comic book you were tweeting about last week!" it's the greatest thing in the world. Because it saves me from having to stand in the corner awkwardly, drinking all the Sprite, and then leaving after ten minutes without saying good-bye to the host. (That's called an Irish exit, and I'm part Irish, so it's part of my genetic wheelhouse.) As someone who had few or . . . yeah, NO friends when I was growing up? Pretty sweet deal.

So how did I get this super-awesome career? Well, you're in luck, because this book is designed to tell you how I got here! Short answer:

A) By being raised weird.
B) By failing over and over again.
C) And by never taking "no" for an answer.

This isn't a typical lady memoir. I appreciate my beauty sleep too much to have crazy "one night in Cabo" stories. I don't have emo ex-boyfriends to gossip about. And I haven't been on any quirky drug trips that ended in profound self-realizations. Guess I'll get busy in those areas for the next book. (Send in the prosecco! That's alcohol, right?)

There will be video game references galore, and at one point you may say to yourself, "This book might be too nerdy even for ME." But the heart of my story is that the world opened up for me once I decided to embrace who I am—unapologetically.

My story demonstrates that there's no better time in history to have a dream and be able to reach an audience with your art. Or just be as weird as you want to be and not have to be ashamed. That lesson's just as legit.

Between the jokes and dorky illustrations (I'm addicted to Photoshop), I hope you can find a teensy bit of inspiration for your own life—to take risks and use all the tools at your fingertips to get your voice out there while you're still not a corpse. Be who you are and use this new connected world to embrace it. Because . . .

We are born an empty bookshelf.

Life is what we fill it with.

HAVEANICEDAY!

Okay, turn the page. Let's get this over with.

1

Why I'm Weird

A brief survey of an eccentric,
homeschooled childhood.

For the record, I was homeschooled for hippie reasons, not God reasons. And it wasn't even *full* hippie. There was no "communal family in an ashram" sort of thing, which is SO disappointing. I've always wanted a glamorous messed-up childhood like that. Raised without clocks. Around kids named Justice League and Feather. Winona Ryder had that, right? She's so pretty.

Nope, I had a middle-class hippie upbringing. More hippie-adjacent than anything. We recycled before it was cool and wore "Save the Whales" T-shirts and . . . that's about it. Oh, and my mom fed us carob instead of chocolate and gave us vitamins that made our breath smell weird. But since my brother and I weren't around other kids that often, we didn't realize the breath thing until *way* later. (Pro tip: put the pills in the freezer to avoid vitamin B mouth stink.)

Before being educated at home (i.e., sequestered in social isolation for nearly a decade), I went to a few different elementary schools from the ages of five to seven. There, I learned several important things about myself:

A) If a boy has an accent, I will fall in love with him. If he has an accent *and* glasses, I will want to marry him. (That means you, Charlie with the Scottish brogue from preschool. You could have had *all of me*. Fool.)

B) I am never going to be passionate about only one subject, unless you count "teacher's suck-a-butt" as a category. I learned early in life that being perfect is a HIT with adults. Who gave special gifts to her kindergarten teacher Miss Julie on every holiday, including Presidents' Day, even though it technically isn't a gift holiday? This girl!

C) I will never be the popular one. That's for girls who wear hair bows that match their dresses and hang out with *other* girls who wear hair bows that match *their* dresses. Back in the late '80s, the hair bow was the rich girl's scrunchie. I had no hair bows *or* scrunchies because we were poor and shopped at Goodwill, and my mom cut my hair in the shape of a salad bowl.

Lastly:

D) The popular girls would never acknowledge that I was destined for respect and high status, so I was happy to go, "Screw
those chicks!" and become the leader of the class misfits. Al-
bino boy? Girl with lisp? The "slow one"? Join my gang! We'll
show the cute bow-girls how much more fun it is to play
dodgeball when you're not worried about that expensive outfit that makes you look all rich and adorable! (Not that I was
jealous.)

Me and my first-grade group were TOTAL *Breakfast Club*: Zoe
from Puerto Rico, who owned a guinea pig; Marcus with curly red
hair, who always smelled like milk; and Megan with the walleye, who
I didn't really want to spend time with, but my mom made me, and
then the kid grew on me because she always seemed delighted by my
company.

We'd hang out in the corner of the homeroom, the corner of
the playground, the . . . generally we hid in corners, defying every-

one with our independence and stuff. Like sharing our sticker books *amongst ourselves only*. (Those popular bitches <u>never</u> saw my Pegasus page, and it was EPIC.) Once, we even stood at the back fence of the school grounds, near the freeway access road, and made the "honk" noise at passing trucks, even though it was *technically against the rules. Oooh!* Since I had an "in" with the teachers, I told my crew, with all the sincerity of Gregory Peck leading a platoon into a World War II battle, "Don't worry, guys. I've got your backs." Being a leader was nerve-wracking, but with responsibility comes great admiration.

So I was fine with it.

It seemed like I was laying the groundwork to become a well-rounded, appearance-aware but antiestablishment woman. A future Susan Sontag, no doubt. Unfortunately, a few life hiccups threw the whole "growing-up-around-other-kids" plan into the emotional meat grinder.

[Jesus Loved Me!]

For second grade, I transferred to a conservative Lutheran elementary school. We weren't religious, but Mom had gone to public school as a child, and the only stories she told us about her education were about kids not wearing shoes to class and the time where she had to shave her head because of lice. Oh, and something about "knocking up" people too early, which I didn't understand, but she was very specific: it ruined women's lives.

Saints Academy was the best school in the cosmopolitan town of Huntsville, Alabama (Home of Space Camp, repreSENT!), and I loved it, except that we had to attend chapel *every day*. I considered this hour a threat to my intellect, because Mom always said, "I don't

want you or your brother becoming a Deep South Bible Thumper."
I took her warning literally. A woman named Ms. Rosemary led reli-
gion class, and whenever she'd touch the Bible with the SLIGHTEST
velocity, I would fold my arms and scowl. "No *way*, lady! You're not
turning me into a 'Thumper!' "

The only thing that got me through the daily service was a big
Jesus statue hung behind the church pulpit. I thought his face, although a little depressed about being up on the cross like that, was
kinda hunky. So I sat there every day, tuning Ms. Rosemary out like
the trombones from the *Peanuts* cartoons, imagining me and J.C.
cuddling in front of the television while we watched *Family Ties* or
Scooby-Doo together. Sometimes we'd even go to Disneyland on our
imaginary honeymoon. J.C. hated Goofy and loved the teacup ride
the best, just like I did. We were the perfect pair in my dreams!

But after a few months, my crush on Mr. Christ transferred to
a Mr. Hasselhoff from *Knight Rider*, and after that I prayed to my
ex-boyfriend's dad for *anything* to get me out of the daily religious
misery. Ms. Rosemary was not a good communicator, and whoever
these "John," "Matthew," and "Judas" people were, they were NOT
HAVING A GOOD TIME. How could I escape?!

And one day, it happened. Ms. Rosemary and a guy named
"Timothy One" gave me the key. After school, I ran into the kitchen.
I couldn't wait to throw my match into the parental tinderbox.

"Mom! Mom! Guess what? They burned money in church today!"

My mother stopped making her hemp yogurt or whatever other
disgusting health food she used to force-feed us. "What?!"

"Yeah, they set *fire to money*. Ms. Rosemary said it's the devil's
paper!"

"Are you kidding? How much?"

"*Hundreds of dollars!* More than any money I've seen in my life!" It was actually a handful of fives, but the dramatic inflation seemed appropriate. And they *did* burn American currency in front of a bunch of seven-year-olds. That part was true. The flames reflected in Ms. Rosemary's eyes. Even my ex-boyfriend Christ looked creeped out, and he was a statue.

My mom went through the roof, just like I knew she would. She's a lovely woman, but cross her about something she cares about, like politics or discontinuing a face cream she loves, and her attitude is, "I will fight you. Right in this department store, throw it down NOW, Clinique associate bitch!"

Her temper could be intimidating, but in this instance, channeling it was in my best interest. And therefore, the BEST!

"Do I have to go to chapel again, Mom?"

"Absolutely not! Don't worry, baby. I'll take care of it." Ooh! The Thumpers were gonna get in TROUBLE!

The next morning, my mom went in to talk with the principal. She put on her special dress, the Liz Claiborne with the sleeves puffed up like the Hindenburg, so I knew she was serious about saving me. While I waited for her to come home, I fantasized about how I'd use my free hour at school. Organize my sticker album or tend to my vast My Little Pony herd. You know, things that would contribute to my future.

But when she returned home a few hours later, her big puffy sleeves were deflated. The school wouldn't apologize for the money burning, and for some crazy reason, they wouldn't make an exception to their curriculum for an outraged partial-hippie family. I couldn't believe it didn't work! I mean, when Mom was upset about things, like my refusing to eat chicken liver, it was *scary*. What was wrong with these people?!

"So I have to go back to chapel again?"

"No. You're not going back to that school at all."

"Cool! Wait, huh?!"

Yup. The Money Burning Incident of 1985 got me yanked out of school completely. Oops.

I briefly got put into another school that was into "unschooling." I can't remember much about that place except it closed abruptly and stole all our money. Adult problems. At the same time, my dad got orders to move from Huntsville, Alabama, to the *Deeper* South—Biloxi, Mississippi—to finish his medical training for the military. And that's when the shit hit my educational fan.

To most of you outside the Deep South, Alabama or Mississippi? It's the same. I mean, they're ass-to-ass anyway. Might as well combine them and make a super hick state, right? But to my Southern extended family, it was bad. They thought we were moving to an antebellum wasteland. My dad was a Yankee himself, so he was even *more* concerned. (Everyone north of Kentucky was referred to as a Yankee in my mom's family. It took me years to realize that wasn't official.)

There wasn't a tradition in our family to homeschool, but there *was* a tradition to get super-mega educated, especially on my mom's side. My grandfather had a PhD in nuclear physics and a thick Southern drawl like molasses. He would invent a desalination machine one week and chew out anyone who distracted him from his favorite Nashville sketch show, *Hee Haw*, the next. "Get outta there, Pooch! You're blockin' Skeeter Davis!"

My grandmother is a scientist, too, and a nurse and an artist and . . . I'll be honest, kinda scary. She once found a dead owl on the side of the road and put it in the back of her pickup in order to analyze the skeleton after it decomposed. I mean, that's kind of Beth Henley interesting behavior, but seeing a dead owl in the back of a pickup is super creepy when you're seven years old, guys. Because you start to suspect that if it were legal, Grandma would do the same thing with your corpse, too.

In order to keep the brain legacy up, my mom scrambled to find schooling options for me and my brother before we moved, but the Gulf Coast of Mississippi didn't have much to choose from. In fact, it had one of the worst education systems in the country, and the only secular private school in the area was a place that made kids wear uniforms, which Mom considered fascist. So we were in a quandary. And because my dad was working twenty-eight hours a day to become a surgeon (scrubs were the only thing I saw him in from the age of eight on), it was up to my mom to figure out an alternative.

So, in a natural leap, she decided to Bob-Vila-DIY our educations herself.

[Home Is Where . . . It All Is!]

In retrospect—and not to be mean to anyone who parented me—it doesn't seem like there was a clear plan going into the whole home-schooling thing. At first, the idea was to follow a comprehensive third-grade curriculum that my mom sent off for in the mail, 1-800 style. It was a system missionary families used when they took their children abroad, and I was a fan of that idea, because it seemed *super* romantic. I'd always dreamed about traveling overseas on a ship like the *Titanic*, and missionaries seemed tragic and special (not like dumb Ms. Rosemary).

Also, homeschooling seemed like something an orphan would do, and I really wanted to be an orphan. Because let's be real: they have it *so good* in kids' literature! They're sad but special, people love them against all odds, and they're always guaranteed a destiny of greatness. *The Secret Garden*, *The Wizard of Oz*, *Harry Potter*? Orphanhood was a bucket list item for me! Along with being able to communicate telepathically with my dog. Based on the loose association of "no school" and "no parents," I was pro-homeschooling. Without understanding what the hell it really was.

On the first day of my new educational life, several boxes of books arrived at our house. Weirdly, all the texts were designed the same, with the words "Science" and "Math" on the covers, like boxes on a generic food aisle.

Despite the weirdo curriculum, I was psyched. And so was my mom.

"You guys ready to learn outside the box?" She lifted up the thick "teaching manual" that she was supposed to use daily. (I don't think it ever got its spine cracked.)

"Yeah!" My brother, Ryon, and I jumped up and down, way too excited, like we were in the audience for a Nickelodeon show. We were ready! Screw the establishment! We were learning on our own!

The next morning I put on pants (even though I didn't technically have to because I was in my own home), sat down with my new books at my "desk" (the kitchen table we fed the cats on), and got ready to rock my brain!

Just to be clear, my mom did make an actual effort to start our day at 9:00 a.m. sharp and do schoolwork until about 1:00 p.m., before "do whatever you want, kids" time. This lasted for maybe a week. With no one to supervise *any* of us, slowly but surely, the family wake-up time slid to a nebulous "midmorning." After a few months, we'd miss all studying before lunchtime because we ate out every day (eating at home was for oppressing housewives), and the restaurants filled up around one, so it was better to leave the house at noon to beat the work crowd. And if we got up around 10:30, that meant . . . I mean, showering is a thing that takes time, guys.

Any structure in our lives disintegrated. "Can the doodles in the margins of my geology chapter count as art class? Really? Thanks, Mom!" Schooling became "We'll get to it later!" around other, more important things, like grocery shopping and going to see the midnight *Rocky Horror Picture Show* screenings. Eventually, my brother and I were on our own. No rules, no tests, and no pesky governmental supervision for children who had recently relocated and weren't on official census lists.

I don't mean to imply that Mom was completely hands-off with our educations. She did stuff. When she got interested in something, she'd say, "Let's go learn about history!" and we'd jump in the car and drive around the state for a few days visiting all the Civil War memorial sites. (It's super fun to roll down a grassy hill where thousands of Confederate bodies are buried.) She'd also yell "Study!" a lot from her bedroom while watching *The Sally Jessy Raphael Show*, and during the first Iraq war she made us start learning Arabic because, "You never know what will happen."

There was, however, one big rule that was enforced during our free-for-all education: We were expected to read. Constantly. All day, every day. Whatever we wanted at the library, the used bookshop, adult or kid section, anything that didn't have nudity or Stephen King on the cover, we could read.

Naturally, I became obsessed with detective pulp fiction. Perry Mason was my favorite. Not the actor who played him in the TV show, Raymond Burr. I hated him; he was bulky, and his skull looked creepy underneath his skin. No, my Perry Mason was taller and debonair, like Cary Grant, or my second love, David Hasselhoff. I collected all but one of the Perry Mason books (*The Case of the Singing Skirt* eluded me; it was my collection's white whale), and I arranged all eighty-one of them by publishing chronology on a makeshift bookshelf in the back of my closet. Because of their influence, my life's dream became clear: to enter the glamorous profession of "secretary," like Perry's loyal companion, Della Street. Either that or "moll"— whatever that job entailed.

THE CASE OF THE
HOMESCHOOLED VIXEN

COMPLETE &
UNABRIDGED

I was also expected to work hard on math, for my grandpa. Since he was a physicist, he would quiz me on equations when we'd go back to Alabama for our monthly visits. My mom liked to impress him. And I did, too, because he always gave me hard candy when I got something right.

"Tell me the Pythagorean theorem."

"A squared plus B squared equals C squared?"

"That's my girl! Now have a Werther's and scoot to the kitchen. *Hee Haw*'s on."

According to my mom, there was a pressing urgency for me to learn as much math as I could. An uncredited study she read once said, quote, "Girls become really stupid in science after they get their period, so you'd better learn as much as possible before that happens." I had such anxiety about this "clearly proven" biological fact that I was studying calculus by the age of twelve. When I finally got my period, I cried, not because I was growing up, but because I had just learned derivatives and really enjoyed doing them. I was scared that estrogen would wipe the ability to do them from my brain.

I guess at a certain point, my dad expressed concern or something about our education. My brother and I didn't see what the fuss was. I mean, we were FINE with doing whatever we wanted and not being forced to "study" like the rest of the world's plebes. But to add structure to our lives, my mom shifted her focus, like any smart businessperson, to outsourcing. Our lives became nothing but lessons.

Ballet, tap, jazz dance, youth orchestra, martial arts, watercolor at the local community college (me and a bunch of eighty-year-olds rockin' the stand of maple trees!), cross-stitch, poise class (held in the back of a department store, for REAL!), my mom basically trained me to become a geisha. With dance lessons alone, I went to class at least three hours a day. Big calves, you are mine for life. So even though it was weird and thoroughly uncomprehensive, my brother and I got an education. Of a sort.

Here's an average daily schedule to give you some perspective about a weekday in my eight- to sixteen-year-old life:

8:00 a.m.: Wake up before everyone and SHUT YOUR CLOCK UP OR ELSE.

8:30 a.m.: *Lost in Space* reruns while eating Rice Krispies.

9:30 a.m.: Math for an hour. Maybe a chapter in one of those logic puzzle books with the grids. I loved puzzles, and Mom said they counted.

10:00 a.m.: AMC movie, hopefully a historical one for studying history, hopefully Technicolor, hopefully *Oklahoma!* If not *Oklahoma!*, 50 percent chance of watching VHS tape of *Oklahoma!*. Or a Cary Grant movie. Half-ass read chapter in history book while watching said movie. CHECK!

12:00 p.m.: Family time! Lunch out at restaurant, one of four that saw us so frequently, they kept a table reserved for us. No one ever questioned why we weren't in school. Thanks, society!

2:00 p.m.: Study Latin because Mom thinks it sounds good to tell people we are learning Latin. Most of the time, read Perry Mason book instead, for "literature."

2:30 to 8:00 p.m.: Geisha lessons.

8:00 to 10:00 p.m.: More movies or TV (especially kung-fu movies for PE) while eating either tuna casserole or manicotti (the only two items my mother cooked) or a microwave TV dinner (the one with the postmodern square desserts).

10:00 to 11:00 p.m.: More reading, video games, or maybe some Legos. For my brain-shape skills.

After 11:00 p.m.: Eh. Go to bed whenever.

[Socialization, Maybe? No? Okay!]

Since everyone we met always brought up "What about their socialization skills?" like naggy in-laws, my mom tried to find us like-minded people to hang out with. Problem was, our family's minds weren't like any others. Especially in southern Mississippi.

My brother and I tried to hang out with other homeschooled kids a few times, but in the ass crack of the Bible Belt, parents who kept their kids home were not going to intersect with our liberal points of view. Ever.

At one awkward meet-up, I was hanging out with a girl around my age on the playground. She was wearing a white long-sleeved shirt and an overdress down to her ankles. I kid you not; she looked like a Pilgrim, and her name was Eunice.

I made the first move. Because socialization beggars can't be choosers. "What books do you read?"

"The Bible."

"Have you read *A Wrinkle in Time*? Or Perry Mason, *The Case of the Fan Dancer's Horse*?"

"No. We only read the Bible."

"Oh. You're a Thumper."

"What?"

"Nothing. Wanna swing?"

"I can't. I might show my ankles."

I laughed because I thought she was joking. She wasn't.

After that, my brother and I were in agreement: being alone was better than hanging around those homeschooled weirdos.

So I didn't spend much time with other children as a kid. SUR-PRISE! I actually can't name one best friend I had during those years outside of a group lesson situation. But it's human instinct to connect, and eventually I found someone who would listen to me no matter how weird I was: my little pink diary.

I called myself Leesie as a kid because I guess my family couldn't think of a more unattractive nickname. Oh wait. My grandpa called me Pooch. That one I won't embrace in print.

But the way I wrote to this diary, you'd think I was writing on the mirror to another little girl who existed on the other side of the page.

"Dear Diary, it's been a month since I wrote. I know, I'm a bad friend."

". . . I finished the *Emily of New Moon* books this week, but I mustn't bore you."

"Today's our first anniversary. Happy Birthday to us!"

I confided everything a weird sixth-grader would share with other children and definitely be rejected for in a typical school situation. Big dreams like, "Wouldn't it be neat to go back to 1880 and there wasn't any kidnappers and progress, and the streams and fields and everything were beautiful?"

> Music Day
> DO YOU KNOW WHAT I WOULD
> LIKE MORE THAN ANY THING
> (EXCEPT ENVIORNMENTAL AND BIOLOGICAL
> STABILITY FOREVER) IN THE
> WORLD? I WOULD LIKE TO TRAVEL
> IN TIME LIKE IN QUANTUM
> LEAP. IT WOULD BE SO WONDERFUL!

I made super-serious vows in the margins, like, "Vow: I will never kill an animal if I can help it." "Vow: I will never marry a man for money." "Vow: I will never let my children live in a slum." Real personality-congealing self-work.

My mom was a big political activist, and that rubbed off on me in a big way, too. The diary is awash in bold political statements and social consciousness.

"We have a new president. George Bush and Dennis the Menace for vice president."

Most of all, the diary was a safe zone. A place where I could share my innermost thoughts, work out a semblance of an identity, analyze my likes and dislikes, and work through my relationships, like that with my brother, Ryon, in a thoughtful, mature way.

That little pink diary is a tome for the ages.

My mother wasn't totally blind to the fact that we needed exposure to other kids. She made efforts. But none of them seemed to stick. Probably because my attitude toward other children was like a seventy-year-old spinster's.

"This girl Kate from violin lesson came over and I told her about my books. She doesn't read. Stupid. I won't explaen [*sic*] them to her. She has no imagination."

"We went to eat with Miss Molly's two kids today and they were putting forks on the floor and stepping on them like hoolegans [*sic*]. We also took Samantha (10) who is fat and obnoxious, but nice when she isn't giggling insatatiabley [*sic*]."

"I went to an opera-ballet by myself. Behend [*sic*] me were two 7-year-old giggling brats. Well, gotta go!"

The only kid in real, close proximity to me was Erin, a thirteen-year-old who lived next door. She taught me that owning a trampoline was the most glamorous thing a girl could have, and that jelly shoes were haute couture. I learned all this through spying on her through my bedroom window, because she didn't like me and wouldn't spend any time with me, physically.

Despite our strained relationship (or because of it), I did have strong thoughts about her lifestyle choices.

Then I went on to apologize about criticizing her behavior, because I think my diary started chiding me about my judgmental attitude. Somehow.

Upshot to my bizarre upbringing: I got super-hyper-educated in many odd areas but was pretty lonely for many years. Sometimes achingly so. They say that the root of everything you are lies in your childhood. Every emotional problem, every screwed-up relationship, every misplaced passion and career problem you can blame on the way you were raised. So I can be kinda smug when I say, "Boy, do I have some excuses!"

Sure, I could have avoided a lot of problems as an adult by being raised like everyone else. I might not have had as much performance anxiety, I might be better at maintaining relationships outside of hitting "Like" on a person's Facebook post when they have a baby. But here's the part I unapologetically embrace: My weirdness turned into my greatest strength in life. It's why I'm who I am today and have the career I have. It's why I'm able to con someone into allowing me to write this book. (Hi, Mr. Simon and Mr. Schuster!)

Growing up without being judged by other kids allowed me to be okay with liking things no one else liked. How else could a twelve-year-old girl be so well versed in dragon lore and film noir? Or think it was the height of coolness to be able to graph a cosine equation? Or long to play Dungeons & Dragons but never get the chance until adulthood because her mom saw that one article on how it made you a Satanic basement murderer?

Most school situations would have shamed all those oddball enthusiasms out of me REALLY quick. Those bow-girls would have snubbed me for them, for sure. But during my childhood my fringe interests remained uncriticized, so they bloomed inside of me without self-consciousness until I was out in the world, partially formed, like a blind-baked pie shell. By then it was WAY too late. I was irrevocably weird.

I'm glad I didn't know better than to like math and science and fantasy and video games because my life would be WAY different without all that stuff. Probably "desk job and babies" different. Not that there's anything wrong with babies. Or desks. I mean, I'm sitting at one now, so my analogy really doesn't . . . I didn't mean to insult anyone with those things, I just . . . oh gosh, panic sweats.

Anyway, thanks for all the weirdness, Mom and Dad!

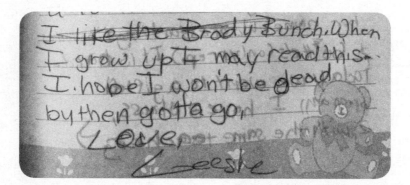

P.S. I don't have a GED. I have two college degrees, but I don't actually have a high school one.

It took writing this chapter to figure that out. Fuck.

2

What Avatar
Should I Be?

Forming my identity with video game morality
tests. And how that led to my first kiss with
a Dragon in a Walmart parking lot.

Knowing yourself is life's eternal homework. (← Another coffee mug
slogan!) We have to dig and experiment and figure out who the hell we
are from birth to death, which is *super* inconvenient, right? And em-
barrassing. Because as teenagers we do all that soul-searching through
our clothing choices. Which we later have photographic evidence of
for shaming purposes. Hippie, sporty, goth, I have an adorable sam-
pling of all my more mortifying phases.

That "mom jeans" picture calls for a postview eye bleaching, huh?

Because I was homeschooled, there are huge holes in my identity that I constantly have to trowel over. Answers to basic, "truth or dare" questions like:

- If you could trade places with one person for a day, who would it be? (I guess Beyoncé because . . . amazing hair reasons?)
- If society broke down, what store would you loot first? (A drug store for tampons? Sorry, dudes, for mentioning tampons in the book.)
- What kind of tattoo would you get? (Um . . . a hummingbird-fairy-dragon creature? Legolas on my right ass cheek? I HAVE NO IDEA, STOP PRESSURING ME!)

I AM covered in the "What superpower would you wish for?" area. I've been asked that question a million times, because, you know, the nerd thing. I would want to be able to speak all languages. I don't even know ONE other language outside of key menu items like "tamale" and "fondue," but whenever I hear a tourist who can't speak English struggling to get directions, I dream of being able to step in, no matter what the language, but especially German since it's emphatic, and fix the problem. Then I accept their thanks with a wave of the hand. *"Es ist nicht, mein freunde!"* In my imagination, I meet a lot of amazing people this way, especially heiresses of castles whom I visit in Europe the following year, anointed as "The American who saved my vacation last summer."

Moving on.

As I grew up, I was bothered more and more by the bigger picture of "Who am I?" Science didn't seem to have much guidance except for one section about personality disorders in my dad's college psychology textbook. And those were a disappointment, because I didn't seem psychotic enough to qualify for any of them. So around the wise old age of twelve, I decided that fortune-telling was the key to learning about who I was. The obsession started with a *Teen Beat* magazine personality quiz, "What perfume are you?" (fruity, BTW, no surprise) and rolled onward from there.

I studied graphology, the art of handwriting analysis, which confirmed that I was an introvert and inspired me to start slanting my words to the right instead of the left. (According to the book, left was the mark of a serial killer.) Numerology, where the letters in your name add up into a single number, told me that I was a "1," which gave me the great excuse to go around saying, "I'm a number one!" I liked that subject a lot. And later, the lost art of phrenology told me that one of my skull bumps was linked to an excess of philobrutism (fondness for pets), which is totally true. My favorite movie is *Babe*, and if you even hum the theme song to it, I WILL start crying. One time I was introduced to James Cromwell, who played a gruff farmer in the movie, and I burst into tears when I touched his hand. Because it was so big and warm and he DANCED FOR HIS PIG.

But out of all the esoteric techniques I played around with, my favorite ended up being Western astrology. Because I loved space. At the time, my TV crush was Commander William T. Riker from *Star Trek: The Next Generation*. He traveled the stars, I was studying them, those things seemed to add up to, "FATE CALLING! DISCOVER WHO YOU ARE SO WE CAN TRAVEL THE GALAXIES TOGETHER, BELOVED ENSIGN!"

At first I was disappointed that I'm a Cancer, and my birthstone is the pearl. I mean, one's a deadly disease, the other is a gem for grandmas. I wanted to be born in October, because opals are the prettiest, but what could I do? My parents did the deed in September. Hello, unfashionable June baby. Aside from those problems, though, everything else was spot-on. My sign said I was a homebody. Check. I was sensitive. Sobbing double check. My Venus was in Taurus, so I would be a constant lover, which I already knew, because I'd read Hawthorne. I understood what happened to ladies with loose garters.

From start to finish, the astrology thing was so convincing that I went ahead and let the rules of Cancerdom become the rules of my life. I started doing all the chores for the cats and dogs because I was a "nurturer." Whenever I got into a fight with my brother, I'd scream, "I can't help it! You crossed into my COMFORT ZONE!" Of all the recommended Cancerian jobs, I settled on "antique dealer," and started collecting books on pottery patterns from the 1920s in order to get a head start on my future career.

"Mom, for Christmas I want this Roseville calla lily vase. The pattern is just MARVELOUS."

I yearned to spread my new cosmic knowledge to other people in my life. Which . . . weren't many. My only option beyond my brother (who was SO Leo) were the girls I knew in ballet class. We'd exchanged words while waiting to do piqué turns across the floor a few times, so we were pretty much besties. I brought my astrology books with me to my next lesson and, in between tap class and pointe class, tried to transform a few fellow young lives.

"Heather, you're a Libra, so your struggle will mostly be with vanity and validating yourself outside your looks."

"Stop saying you'll never be able to do three pirouettes, Jackie! You're an air sign; it's totally gonna happen!"

"Will you pass history class? Oooh, you're a Pisces with the moon in . . . ugh. Give it up, Tina."

Turns out the girls loved having their own private psychic in the changing room. I convinced my mom to drop me off at class a half hour early for "stretching" and started consulting with all the dancers on parental problems, summer school plans, you name it. A lot of them brought in birthdays of boys they liked in order to see how their charts aligned. I'm pretty sure my advice led to a few de-virginizations. It was an awesome change from no one wanting to talk to the weird homeschooled girl! I'd finally found a way to relate to other kids. It was fulfilling. And made me popular. And eventually I got shut down.

Miss Mary, my dance teacher, stopped me one day when I arrived. "Felicia, what are you carrying?"

"Um, just a few books." There were fifteen stacked up to my chin. I'd just discovered Chinese astrology and I Ching and couldn't wait to tell Jennifer about the guy she crushed on, Simon. Sadly, his stubborn Tiger traits would always keep them apart.

"Megan's mom doesn't like her learning about astrology. I'm going to have to ask you to stop talking about it with the girls."

"But it's the science of the stars!"

"She thinks it's Satanic. You gave her daughter a pentagram."

"It's a *natal* chart, duh. You can't let ignorance trump *science* here, Miss Mary!"

Nothing I said could persuade her. She was a Taurus. Once her mind was made up, it was over.

I was forced to hang up my crystal ball, and eventually the girls stopped talking to me again. (And they probably made terrible life choices they could have avoided if they hadn't been deprived of my insight, thanks to Megan's mom.) I was upset but soon bounced back and was able to move on to another, more accessible place for friendship and identity exploration: the online world.

[Vidya Gamez!]

I don't need a psychologist to tell me that my love of role-playing games is linked to my childhood quest for self. Link number two: I like killing virtual monsters.

We were always big on technology in my family. My dad studied to be an engineer before becoming a doctor, and he's the kind of dude who always had a PalmPilot in a large holster attached to his belt. (Now he has his Android phone in a large holster attached to his belt, but that's his life choice, and I will not mock it. To his face.)

When I was about seven or eight, my grandfather gave us his secondhand "laptop," which was as big as a dining room table.

I think it was meant to help my parents with their college courses, but generally my mom set the standard for us kids by playing video games on it. They were text-only, because the monitor didn't support graphics, so it was more like reading an interactive novel than anything. The gaming equivalent of liking weird foreign films with subtitles.

1986 "Laptop"

My favorite one to watch her play was called Leather Goddesses of Phobos. It came with a scratch-and-sniff sheet tied to various parts of the game, and I sniffed the pizza area until it disappeared, even though it smelled more like dog food than pepperoni. (If I did drugs, I would totally be a sniffer. Gasoline and Magic Markers, I gotta fight against getting my nose all up in there.) After watching my mom type "attack Tiffany with pipe" and having the game tell her back, "Tiffany yells, 'ow!',", I knew I was hooked on video games for life.

As my brother and I grew up, we played any PC computer game we could trick our parents into buying us. It was the primary hobby we used to fill our many, MANY free hours between geisha lessons.

"We need this program called Math Blaster to help us learn better, Mom. Oh, and those four other games under it, too. Don't look too close!"

In an amazing stroke of Cancerian fate, right after the ballet class Satan-worshiping situation, I stumbled upon a video game series called Ultima. Besides pretty much being one of the seminal Role-Playing Game series of ALL TIME (don't argue with me about this, you're wrong), this is a video game that literally changed my life.

What set this series apart from other indecipherably pixilated games of the early '90s was the way you created your character. At the beginning of the game, a fortune-teller asks you several multiple-choice questions like:

"A girl is to be killed for stealing bread from a dying woman. What do you do?"

A) Let them kill her; she deserved it.

B) Demand that she be freed; her crime is understandable.

C) Offer to take the punishment instead. She's hot.

(Okay, that wasn't one of the real questions.)

Depending on the way you answered, your avatar (the character you played; don't worry: I'll hold your hand through the nerd lingo) started the game differently. Your decisions influenced who you were in the world; your morals shaped what Virtues (like Honesty and Courage) you were aligned with. Let me simplify: As a kid, this video game SAW INTO MY SOUL. It defined me, then projected me into a world where I could be a virtual hero version of myself. I could walk around alone, without my mom warning me there were molesters waiting to kidnap me on every corner. I could go shopping and steal things and kill monsters! Oh, and I could name my avatar AFTER MYSELF! Screw astrology, I was in love!!!!!

I played the games in the Ultima series for HOURS and HOURS a day, month after month. I decided it checked the box for many subjects in my homeschooled curriculum, like computer science, literature, and PE (for the eye-hand coordination). The only thing my mom ever said about it was, "I'm glad you're concentrating on something, kids!"

I became completely immersed in the world, channeling my avatar's ruling Virtue of "Compassion" everywhere in the 16-bit realm. And deep down, all I wanted IN THE WORLD was to talk to other people about it. Discuss how bitchin' the graphics were. How awesome the lore was. And *Holy crap, this game allows you to BAKE VIRTUAL BREAD!* I NEEDED to share this joy with other humans! But the girls at ballet had no clue what a computer was (Megan's stupid mom probably thought that technology was the work of Satan), and my brother was . . . my brother. I mean, brothers are practically subhuman, right? No, I needed real live people who loved this Ultima game who were not living in my house with me! Where could I find them?!

Hmmmm . . .

[Technology-ships]

BONG-BOOP-BOOP-BEEP-BEEP-BOOP-BOOP-BEEP
\<PAUSE\>
PLAP PLEEP PLWAAAAAAANG SCREEEEWAAAAAA
KLEEEEEEEEEEEEEEEEEEEEEEESHWAAAANG GLAW CEGLAW
SSCHHEHEHHEHEHHHHHHHHHHHWHHHHHHHHH
\<STATIC\>

Just approximating that sound in type makes me recall joy, like other kids getting excited over the creepy tinkle of an ice cream truck. In my childhood world, the sound of a modem dialing up to connect with another computer was the sound of freedom.

I'm probably a member of the oldest generation that grew up with the idea that you can connect with other people using a computer. My grandfather worked for the military, where he headed the nuclear physics laboratory at the US Missile Command for twenty years, so he was probably sending groovy selfies back and forth with colleagues in the '70s. When the commercial internet started to emerge in the '80s, he encouraged my parents to get on the computers-talking-to-other-people train earlier than 99 percent of the rest of the population. And we thought we were soooo cool.

There was only one commercial online company at the time, CompuServe, and it was not sophisticated, guys. It was the cave painting equivalent to Tumblr. I mean, you had to pay $10 an hour to use it. That's right, in ye olden internet days, kids, people had internet cafés in their own living rooms! But, for the times, CompuServe had it all. It offered news, messaging, and bulletin boards covering every subject you'd want to chat about in a glorious "only text" interface. Oh, and tons of racy ASCII porn.

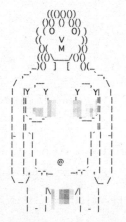

HEY BABY. DIAL ME UP.

For that, and many reasons, it was a long time before my brother and I were allowed to log online by ourselves. We could only pop on and off to get quick hints about video game puzzles we were too lazy/stupid to figure out on our own. (Conservative usage of CompuServe was more affordable than using the 1-888 hint line, which we previously used to run up $400 phone bills. We got very good at hiding the mail from my father.) But eventually, when I was about fourteen, my family graduated online technologies to a newer online service called Prodigy. Which was revolutionary amazing because it charged $12.95 for unlimited use. In addition, it had REAL GRAPHICS. Like, eight whole colors.

In 1994, this interface looked like virtual reality.

Prodigy had online GAMES and interactive bulletin boards, and did I mention it was a flat rate, so my brother and I could use it as long as we wanted and not get in trouble? This was like Prometheus rolling into town, "Here, humans, check out this fire thing." It changed everything!

As soon as I got access, I immediately went to the message boards to search the video game discussions and found a group called the Ultima Dragons. Browsing through the posts, I couldn't believe it.

I had finally found a place where people totally knew what I was talking about when I wrote, "OMG ULTIMA IS THE BEST GAME OF ALL TIME SORRY FOR THE CAPS!" My dreams about finding a place to create true, meaningful friendships around my fake video game world had come true.

And my mom didn't have to drive me anywhere!

I joined the club and named myself Codex Dragon because everyone had a Name + Dragon theme going on, and a Codex was an object in the video game that represented the "book of infinite wisdom." Are some of you feeling like it's getting too geeky in here? You probably should have read the book blurb better, because I'm just getting STARTED.

As a member of the Ultima Dragons, we didn't just post about the games, although a majority of the stuff was, "How do you defeat the stupid gargoyles at the Shrine of Humility because I keep dying!" We talked about movies we loved and books we read. The people who shared my love of Robert Jordan's The Wheel of Time fantasy book series immediately became my closest friends. They were the first people I'd ever met who'd read them, too. (Although I was the only one who had all the hardbacks in first edition and did a yearly reread. Impressed? Well, THEY were.)

It might sound dorky, but the Ultima Dragons gave me my first environment where I could express my enthusiasms freely to my peers. Hell, for once I HAD peers. And I mined it for all it was worth. Socially, artistically. In all ways. Even . . . with poetry.

Yes, I wrote poems dedicated to a video game—shut up with the judgment (although it's warranted). The following is a really special example. It's an ode to one of the fictional characters in Ultima video game. A jester. His name was Chuckles.

> Merry bells tinkling loud
>
> Inane smile he wears quite proud
>
> Juggling spheres of pink and blue,
>
> Dancing nimbly on pointed shoe.
>
> His antics made to draw a smile,
>
> foolish murth conceals sly guile.
>
> As purpose proud to entertain
>
> he also gives your Avatar a royal pain!

Hand me the Pulitzer. Dozens more where that came from!

There was also a separate message board called the "Drunken Stupor" where we'd post what I now understand to be "fanfic" set in a tavern (called the Drunken Stupor) *about* our Ultima Dragons characters. Meaning, ourselves. Example:

> Codex Dragon enters the tavern with a tough look on her face. Busting open the door with her high-heeled boot, then she strides over to the bar and then slams down her silver sword of Grandia. She looks at Tempest Dragon with torrid eyes, "You! I don't know whether to kill or kiss you." Tempest looks up. Like he wants her to do both.

Looking back, there's an uncomfortable dose of S&M in the stories I wrote at fourteen. I attacked other Dragon members with swords and whips a lot, and Codex always wore sexy leather outfits with stiletto heels. The guys LOVED how creative I was! Their feedback on the stories made me discover that flirting was fun. So I proceeded to do it with a lot of people.

Um, pretty much everyone.

You gotta understand I had NO OTHER GUYS in my life! Sure, there were some boys in my dance classes and community theatre productions I acted in, but the other chorus members of *Brigadoon* didn't generally put their Ps in Vs. The guys online were into girls, and I had access to them. Do the teen math: *I wanted all of them.*

We started sending pictures to each other (physically in the mail, yes), which either fueled or quashed the fire of awkward teen romance. I got a ton of positive feedback on my submission:

This picture was originally taken for a JCPenney modeling competition. I was not a winner in the eyes of the department store, but the Dragons all thought I was a treasure.

Yes, those are velvet high-tops.

I got pictures back in exchange, and it was weird to put a face to an online personae. They never matched up the way I imagined. The asshole goth punk of the group turned out to be a Midwestern blond guy in a football outfit, straight out of *Friday Night Lights*. The friendliest of the group turned out to be a little person, which was a shock, but then cool, and no one brought it up again. Several of the other guys had really long stringy hacker hair, or were old, so I stopped flirting with them (kinda), and two standouts got my thumbs-up endorsement for continued romantic flirty times.

On the one hand, Wolf Dragon's picture was a Sears portrait special, with the bokeh-blurred edges, and a splattering of pubescent facial hair, erratically spread, like a limp hair-gun had shot follicles at his face. But I liked his personality online, and he had kind eyes that overcame the velvet waterfall behind him. I was into him for his brain, mostly. And his cat named Poe.

Camouflage Dragon, on the other hand, was, by Dragon standards, the hottie. He did have a significant unibrow, but he had eyes the color of a tiger's eye gem, ochre and deep, and he was into math, which I liked because my grandpa would approve. I gave myself permission to get a crush on him, too.

I wasn't ready to commit to one boy or the other fully, I wanted to keep both in the romantic-type running, so we became an online trio, sending messages back and forth to one another in private email boxes. We also sent handwritten letters snail-mail style filled with song lyrics. Mostly Bangles and Aerosmith.

"Camouflage, I like the idea we could all go to the same college. That would be so cool, but I don't wanna hope too hard. Like Steven Tyler says,

You're callin' my name, but I gotta make clear
I can't say, baby, where I'll be in a year."

We would three-way call every other night. The guys each lived in different parts of New Jersey, and I remember thinking, *Wow, their accents are so exotic.* We mostly talked about the Ultima games, but we got into other things, too. Like . . . other video games. Our conversations were always fraught with veiled sexual innuendo. "What kind of armor do you hope your character wears in Ultima VIII, Codex? What kind of corsets?"

My mom was cool with all of this, by the way. She had recently gotten more defensive about our socialization; maybe the state started checking in on us? Who knows? But she was extra aggressive in supporting my relationships with all my online Dragon friends, especially the romantic ones. After all, SHE first had sex at sixteen and other details I tried to black out after she shared them.

The summer of my fifteenth birthday, my family had to move to Louisville. And because we were going in the general compass direction of New Jersey-ish-ness, Mom decided that it would be okay to take a trip and see as many of my Ultima Dragon friends as I wanted. Yes! MEET-UP TIME!

I was so excited; I'd never been above the Mason-Dixon Line (yes, Southern people still had that as a THING) and I was going to meet face to face with my only friends in the world and perhaps a potential husband. My mom and brother would be along for the ride to cramp my style . . . but whatever. For my romantic teenaged heart, this was do-or-die time. I was gonna figure out which one of these guys I liked better if it KILLED ME!

New Jersey is much farther north than you'd think if you're driving from Alabama in a two-door Acura hatchback with broken air conditioning. We arrived at Camouflage's house after a few days (for a real name, let's call him Tyler. Which was hard to remember in person anyway, to NOT call him Camouflage). And when we got there it was obvious he hadn't explained everything about the meet-up to his mom. Or . . . anything.

We were shoved in the basement with the four other Dragons who showed up while Tyler got chewed out by his parents upstairs.

muffled yelling "Weirdos!"

"Mom!" *muffled yelling* "NOT weirdos!"

That went on for a while. Meanwhile, we made the best of it downstairs and awkwardly tried to pin faces to Dragon usernames.

There was Aeire, our club leader, with waist-length blond hair and a slacker vibe, who never took his sunglasses off, and his girlfriend, Mist Dragon, who looked like she should be into reading romance novels, not killing gargoyles. I don't think I ever got either of their real names, but they were nice and came from Ohio, which was also an exotic state to me. "You eat spaghetti with your chili? How interesting!"

There were a few older dudes who I can't remember much of at all because my mom was kind of a cock block to us interacting. And thankfully, Wolf (fake real name Henry) had shown up from exotic EAST New Jersey for my inspection.

He approached me, wearing that Sears portrait smile. "Hey!"

"Hey! Wow, weird to meet you in person!"

Insert awkward attempt at hug. Abandon.

Insert awkward pause.

And another.

I sat down next to him on a slightly broken futon, and within twenty seconds I could feel the possibility of romance disappearing. Instant turn-off. A never-gonna-happen-let's-be-friends-forever switch flipped in my head. And it wasn't because of his looks (although his picture didn't translate BETTER in person), but there was just no chemistry there. He was someone I got along with and wanted to talk hours to on the phone. But have my virgin intercourse with? Nope.

I don't think the attraction disappeared for him as instantaneously as it did for me, so I had to navigate the dance of trying to reframe our relationship as friends and not phone flirt mates before my other courtier, Tyler, got finished being yelled at upstairs by a very angry New Jersey woman. (By the way, her accent was NOT exotic.)

"How's your cat doing?"

"Good! I can't believe I'm seeing you in person. You're so prett . . ."

"Look over there! A washer-dryer combo! Cool!"

I tried to throw the conversation to the group as a whole, but at a certain point, the whole vibe in the basement got SUPER stilted. No one felt comfortable enough to share personal information. We'd followed a mad impulse to connect in person, and the experience was NOT equaling the anticipation we felt. I think we all had completely different ideas of one another in our heads. Also, a few of us were CHILDREN, and I don't think that sunk in over the computer monitors as well as it did in real life. We tried to circle safe topics like, "Can you believe what Periwinkle Dragon said about Feather Dragon on the forum last week . . ." but after that, everything trailed off into tense pauses. It was extremely uncomfortable.

For once in my life, I can say, "Thank goodness my mom was there!" She has a talent for prompting inappropriate conversations with strangers. As soon as she took charge, we learned about people's divorces, sexual orientation, and we were just getting into drug use confessions and my yelling, "Mom!" really loud when Tyler came downstairs and suggested we "Go out for a walk and a bite to eat."

Translation: His mom was booting the weirdos.

The group moved down to the Jersey boardwalk, which is lovely and has excellent taffy, and we made a beeline for the video game arcade, where all the Dragons proceeded to play separately from each other for another two and a half hours, only stopping for a short break to get hot dogs. I spent most of my time with Camouflage (damnit, Tyler!) and tried to salvage the dream of finding my true love in New Jersey.

And, try as I might, it just didn't work. Yes, he was smart and cute in person and clearly hadn't doctored his photos because there was still that unibrow, but the whole package was like seeing a Tiffany box from afar and being so psyched and then getting up close and realizing it's a pack of gum from the 99-cent store. There's an indefinable "something" you have with another person to get your reproductive organs all flame-y, and it just wasn't there with any of the Dragons. I'd had a big crush on Tyler before, but in retrospect, I think it was only because he gave good phone voice.

Getting the romance question out of the way was a relief. Now I could actually have fun! Henry, Tyler, and I proceeded to beat the crap out of each other at Street Fighter and Mortal Kombat. We had an awesome, platonic time together, and I was prepared to leave happy knowing I would still have two great friends online, and I could let my heart move on to other places.

And then my mom jumped in.

She had always been a BIG Tyler fan and decided to get her pom-poms out.

"Isn't he sweet? His mom's a bitch, but he's so cute."

"He's okay, Mom. So is his mom." His mom wasn't okay—what little I saw of her reminded me of a character from *The Godfather*, but I didn't want to get judge-y.

"You two look so good together, his eyes are pretty. You need to get away from the group. Go off alone together! I'll distract Henry."

"What? No, I'm fine!"

"We're leaving in the morning, Felicia. Go down to the beach with him alone!"

"No! That's weird! Why?"

"Felicia, you have to kiss him. This is your chance!"

And then it became clear. Before we left New Jersey, my mom was determined to hook me up.

For the record, I had never kissed a boy before, and she had to know this, since I'd been locked away like Rapunzel. Maybe it was because she drove seventeen hours and wanted some payoff, but she decided to jump in and grease the libido. In her "helpful" mind, I didn't know enough to interact with guys properly, and she was going to be my guide. Whether I liked it or not.

At the end of the afternoon, all the other Dragons dispersed with the promise of "Let's meet up again!" (Except we never would.) Then my mom found an excuse to drive me and Tyler to a nearby Walmart.

She dragged my brother inside, leaving me and Tyler alone in the car together, with the ulterior motive of giving us time to mash faces.

"I'm going to get some snacks for the drive tomorrow. Ryon, you want Bugles?" My brother got out of the car and followed her without looking up from his Game Boy. I don't think he looked up from that thing for six years, to be honest.

I made one last desperate attempt to escape. "We can go with you! Please!"

"Nope. You two stay here and have fun!" As she left, my mom gave me her "You'd better do this, or I'm gonna pinch you really hard later" look through the open car window.

Great. I had to go through with it.

I remember very little of the buildup to my very first kiss. Tyler and I were in the backseat together, and it was hot. Anything we said to each other was white noise as I bathed in my own pubescent sweat and dread. When I think back on it, maybe Tyler thought I was nervous because I was excited to kiss him? For the record, I was not. I just wanted to check the box and get it over with so my family could come back with Bugles.

Finally, I made a move in. He obliged. We met in the middle and . . .

It was not good. The feeling of "Ew" is still vivid now. I remember thinking, *Lips are pretty gross.* In my defense, I am a REALLY careful eater, and his lips were wetter than lips should EVER be when you're out of a pool.

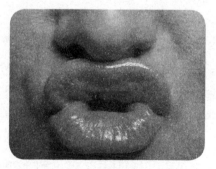

Grody. We retracted, underwhelmed. A few beats of silent horror spanned the back of the 1990 two-door Acura.

"So . . . um, are you gonna write any more Ultima game poetry soon? I think you should do one on the magical explosion at Scara Brae."

"Really? I do love that quest line!"

We talked about the finer points of the game inventory management system until my family returned. Whew, significant sexual life experience, over!

My mom gave me a pointed look in the rearview as she got in the car. I responded by putting my sticky, sweaty hand on Tyler's sticky, sweaty hand and smiled. She nodded and we drove off.

And that is why, to this day, I hate New Jersey.

Even though it wasn't great, that trip didn't cause me to break off my relationship with the Ultima Dragons group. The breakup happened a few months afterward when Prodigy stopped unlimited monthly usage and started charging by the hour. Dumb jerks. The group dispersed, but a few friendships persevered. I kept up my platonic three-way with Tyler and Henry, and Henry actually ended up going to college at University of Texas with me the following year and became one of my best friends. Tyler drifted away because his mom wouldn't let him join us; she thought we were freaks. She was probably right.

I know the story of my Dragon-hood may sound a little sad and weird and super geeky, but (kiss story aside) for a girl who was lonely and desperate for friends, that group of people was the most important social thing to happen to me growing up. I can't imagine being as confident about my passion for geeky things today without that opportunity to connect with OTHER people who were saying, "Wow, I love those geeky things, too!"

That early community taught me how wonderful it is to connect with like-minded people. No matter how lonely and isolated and starved for connection you are, there's always the possibility in the online world that you can find a place to be accepted, or discover a friendship that's started with the smallest of interests but could last a lifetime. Your qualification for finding a place to belong is enthusiasm and passion, and I think that's a beautiful thing.

No one should feel lonely or embarrassed about liking something. Except for illegal sex picture stuff. And murder and dogfighting . . . I'll make a list. It'll be pretty long, now that I think about it. But you get the gist.

Signed,

Codex Dragon

-==(UDIC)==-

- 3 -

Jail Bait

The deprived college years: Surprisingly, people didn't
invite the sixteen-year-old violin prodigy to keggers.

My mother got me into playing the violin at age two and a half because she was watching a morning talk show and saw a bunch of small children playing the instrument together in a perfectly straight line, like creepy toddler robots. They were showing off a technique called Suzuki that teaches kids to play really young, even before they learn how to walk without stumbling around, looking all drunk and stuff. In a startling not-so-coincidence, I was born with a congenitally shortened ligament in my left thumb (I like to think it's a romantic birth defect, like Anne Boleyn's sixth finger), and in my mom's mind, "crooked thumb + violin neck" added up to destiny.

My music studies were a big excuse for my being homeschooled, so I would theoretically have more time to practice and become a world-renowned soloist, traveling around the world in a red velvet coach. Unfortunately, I didn't take it seriously enough to earn the coach, and my parents didn't force me to try. Which I'm thankful for. I've met a lot of those kids whose parents crammed something down their throats trying to make baby geniuses. Even by my maladjusted standards, those kids were maladjusted.

No, the most my mom ever did to pressure me about my violin was scream, "YUCK!" really loudly from the other room if I hit a bad note while practicing.

Laziest stage mom EVER.

I did practice when I was bored, and I was bored a lot, so around the age of eight I started to be able to play without sounding like I was throttling a cat. After that, my mom decided to upgrade me to the best teacher we could get in the haute-cultured Southern Mississippi vicinity. I'm not sure what the endgame was other than "My beautiful child is a violin savant, I will get her the best training possible so the world can be blessed with her greatness!" but it was a real gift, because we didn't have a lot of money and lessons were expensive, and my violin abilities ended up getting me a full scholarship to college. I just wish the teacher she found me at the time hadn't been a Russian madman.

For years, we'd drive an hour and a half to New Orleans so I could train with a huge, had-to-be-related-to-a-bear man named Viktor. He was from the "A touch of abuse very good!" school of Soviet training. He would hit me on the arm when I played off-key. With an *actual stick*. My theory? It was the whittled-down arm bone of a former student.

"*Nyet! Nyet!* You no practice?! Lazy!" He'd throw up his hands and stare at me with colossal disappointment, like I was his underage daughter, pregnant with fifteen sets of twins.

"I'm sorry, I'll practice more next week!" I rarely did, but it always felt good to have that moment of resolve, like saying, "I'm gonna learn French!" It doesn't MATTER if you do it or not, deciding is the high, right?

When I'd massacre Bach again the following week, Viktor would take a more Communist approach. *"Nyet! Nyet!!"* He'd stomp over and take my bow hand roughly from behind me and start sawing at the instrument, moving my arm like a terrified puppet across the strings. I'd hang on as much as I could, struggling to keep the bow anywhere near the instrument.

"Understand? You play like this!" I didn't, but I'd nod and just pray for the horrible amusement park ride to be over. This is how I learned to play the violin really, really well.

Despite Czar Viktor's passive aggressiveness and his exact resemblance to Mikhail Gorbachev (sans head tattoo), I loved him and never wanted to disappoint him. Because, as sad as he could get when I was lazy, he became equally impassioned when I was great.

One year I had to play a Mozart concerto for the spring recital, and I came super prepared for dress rehearsal at Viktor's house. My family was having money problems, and it cost a lot to hire a pianist to play with me, so I was determined to get a gold star to show that the money was worth it. Oh, and because my mom said, "I'm paying a lot of money for that pianist, we might not eat this week, so play well or else!"

We started rehearsing, objectively I was rocking the trills, and in the middle I looked over and saw Viktor waving his arms and head around like Stevie Wonder. (No insult, he was just *into* it.) Out of his right eye, I could have sworn there was . . . moisture? Trickling?! *Was the meanest man I'd ever met having a stroke?! Was I having a stroke? What should I do?!* It freaked me out and I almost stopped playing. I didn't, because I didn't want to waste $2.25 a minute, but the impulse was definitely there.

After I was done, Viktor walked over and cupped my face in both hands like it was a Fabergé egg. "So good, so good, my heart!" He thumped himself in the chest. It was a gesture of . . . I'm not sure. Something positive, like CPR. As the pianist left, he screamed into his kitchen at his little wife, Raeza, who was always cooking while wearing a pair of medical scrubs, even though she wasn't in the medical profession.

"Raeza! Borscht! We eat!"

He hauled me into the kitchen, a room I'd never entered in more than five years of studying with him, and ate disgusting blood-pink soup together.

He looked over the top of his bowl, smiling. "Yes?"

"It's great!" I wanted to throw up.

"Good girl." Viktor patted my head and slurped.

I think in Russia, he'd legally adopted me.

[College Timez!]

When I got into my teens, I took the violin more seriously. Because people would tell me how I was adorable when I played, and I'm a praise monkey. (Will perform for smiles!) I auditioned for the Juilliard pre-program when I was fourteen and was accepted, but finances wouldn't allow us to move to New York City full-time. It was a crushing blow because I was definitely ready to move out of the house. In fact, I was *always* ready to move out. I'd picked out a list of excellent boarding schools by age twelve and couldn't understand why we weren't wealthy enough for me to go abroad like in the "Madeline" books. Or, alternatively, rent me an apartment down the street. I forged my mom's signature and paid all the bills for her anyway, so at that point it was just geographical logistics, right? My parents couldn't understand my vision.

So when my professor offered to help me get into University of Texas at Austin, I was all over it like a rabid dog on jerky. Or whatever analogy. Look, I was excited.

We were living in San Antonio at the time, and my violin teacher was Mr. Frittelli, a professor at UT. He was a tiny man and a dazzling violinist who appreciated a good fart joke. My kind of guy.

One day he asked, "What are you doing for college?"

I sighed a dramatic teen sigh. "I have a ton of them picked out, but I dunno, I have forever to decide." Being precocious was SO HARD.

"How old are you?"

"Fifteen, gonna be sixteen in June."

"Do you want to go to college this year?"

"What?"

OMG.

"Yes. Take me there now, please!"

I'm not sure who Mr. Frittelli blackmailed in order to get an underage teenager with literally NO school transcripts into a public collegiate institution, but a week after we spoke—*BOOM*—he'd arranged for a full scholarship for me to study music starting in the fall. All I had to provide was an SAT score!

Um . . . okay?

I had taken exactly one standardized test in my life. It was an IQ test to get into preschool. I got all the questions right except one where they asked, "Where is your mom in this picture? The beach or the shed?" I answered "the shed" because I thought they meant "the shade." I knew at age five that my mom was paranoid about sun damage, no way was she hanging on the beach. So in a relative sense, I did perfectly. Anyway, whatever qualifications, I was not letting a stupid bubble test get in the way of this "escape homeschooling" opportunity. The SAT was the Rosetta stone for me. I had no idea what was going on with that thing, but I was gonna crack it!

I scheduled the test for the following weekend (five days of study seemed more than enough) and got one of those thick SAT practice books from the library. I filled out more than one hundred practice tests in five days. No joke. Hand cramped, eyes watering; in retrospect, it would have made a great movie montage with "Eye of the Tiger" playing in the background.

If this story followed classic movie plot construction, I would have failed the test horribly, given up, then discovered newfound resolve through an old homeless man's inspirational words to try again and ace the results. But life doesn't follow traditional story arcs. Whether it was by naïveté or the hand of Thor, I have no idea, but when the results came back, I'd gotten an almost perfect score. One of the few answers I missed was a vocabulary question defining "Spartan," which does NOT mean "warrior-like" but "austere and sparse." (To this day I still think that is misleading and stupid. I saw *300*. What am I, a fool?) But based on my scores, I was definitely, absolutely going to college!

Things were going to CHANGE! I could be on my own. To experience life in bigger social contexts than just me and my brother and my online friends! I would move to Austin, be like Felicity or Doogie Howser, MD, plans plans plans . . . TIRE SCREECH.

Turns out, legally, I was too young to live in the dorms alone. My family's solution? Move to Austin so I could attend school while living at home.

And my mom ended up driving me to college every day.

For four years.

Sigh.

I entered college just as I turned sixteen, with a plan to double-major in mathematics and music. The math thing was for my dad and grandpa, who were firm believers in Real Degrees. (I capitalize because that's how they sounded when they said I had to get one. "A Real Degree.")

You'd think jumping into a school of 30,000-plus students would be intimidating for a girl who'd had only her little brother to hang around for most her life, and you would be right. Luckily, most of my time was to be spent in the music building annex, which was a small underfunded island unto itself. So at least it was the shallow end of the pool I got thrown into without having any limbs to swim.

There were only about six hundred students enrolled in the music school, and people rarely left because it was assumed you locked yourself in a 4x4 practice room for eight hours a day or you were "never going to amount to anything as a musician, so why are you taking up room if you're not serious?" No peer pressure or anything. The building sat on the fringes of campus and was supposed to house the next generation of artists. It had the aesthetics of a Hungarian women's prison.

It was cold in the winter and hot in the summer, with elevators that broke all the time. There were long green couches on the first floor that smelled like failure and skin flakes, and no one would nap on them for fear of catching salmonella. I think the whole design was just a nefarious plot to force students back into their tiny LED-lit practice room cages. All senses besides hearing were punished.

I was, of course, nervous about this huge leap into adulthood, so I prepared a detailed strategy for my first day of class. It was mostly inspired by bad TV shows. I would dress as inconspicuously as possible so people wouldn't notice me, and that way I could do recon to figure out my place in the world. Like going undercover in *21 Jump Street*. I would draw NO attention to myself, so no one would see how young or how awkward I was, and eventually, I'd just EXIST, unquestioned. Assimilated, like the Borg. Then, after I'd met everyone and fallen in love with qualified men, I'd get a cute outfit, do my hair, and arrive at school completely made over. The guys would fall at my feet, but the one who was nicest to me when I was plain and boring would have my heart, like that episode of *Beverly Hills, 90210*. Or

Boy Meets World? One of those. Who cares, none of it happened like that, anyway.

First day of class, I wore a huge pair of pleated jeans and a T-shirt that was a men's large and a bigger sweater over it, like a late '80s hip-hop star. Totally inconspicuous. I began college by lurking in corners, acting like the kind of kid people say, "But she was so quiet!" after a school shooting. But by noon, no one had approached me to talk. So far, so good!

Everyone who was enrolled in college orchestra had to audition on the first day of the semester so the conductor could figure out how good you were and what seat to assign you for the season. It was *The Hunger Games* for music majors. The conductor, I'll call him Mr. Murray, was a young upstart who looked like Matthew McConaughey with Farrah Fawcett hair. It tousled around when he worked in the hottest way, waving like American golden wheat. Everyone had a crush on him, and I'm sure he could have slept with every woman in the building (me included), but he was a newlywed with an extremely hot wife who wore a black leather jacket and drove a motorcycle. He didn't need the awkward foreplay of orchestra geeks.

My plan for the audition was to lowball my performance so the other students wouldn't look at me for any reason, but as I entered the room, Mr. Murray said, "It will be nice having you in the orchestra this year. Mr. Frittelli has told me a lot about you."

Sheer panic. Commence inner-anxiety monologue: *Mr. Frittelli told him about me? That means he told him I was good! And if I'm bad, Mr. Frittelli will look bad. But I don't want to be TOO good, or the other kids won't like me. But if I suck, they might take away my scholarship . . . B-U-T . . .* I freaked out inside, torn between fitting in with my peers and being a praise monkey teacher pleaser.

I looked deep into Mr. Murray's cornflower-blue eyes, tried to gather my wits, and in the end, there was no choice. The hot adult wanted me to be good. So I played my heart out.

When the roster got posted that afternoon, I had been placed in the number two First Violin seat. Right in front of the conductor's podium. The Park Place of orchestral real estate, right out of the gate. Crap.

As I looked at the board, I heard a grad student say behind me, "Who the hell is Felicia Day?!" and I slunk away, swimming in my huge acid-washed pants. It was going to be harder to navigate this whole schooling thing than *Saved by the Bell* had ever taught me.

In the following weeks, I tried to keep a low profile, hiding in the back of classes and practicing in the most out-of-the-way dungeon-like practice rooms, but I could tell everyone was curious about me. I looked ten years old, got placed in front of all the seniors and grad students, and I knew they were all thinking, *How good is this kid?*

I caught a few of them eavesdropping outside my practice room door, and rather than make friends, I'd glare through the tiny glass window and stop playing to mark up my music in a real fake-spacework kinda way. The idea that I could open up to them never occurred to me. I wasn't used to humans enough to have organic social impulses.

But as the weeks went by, anxiety started eating me up. I knew I couldn't hide forever. They would hear me, and judge me. I wondered if it was too late to quit college and go back home to hang out with my brother and play Legos. It all came to a head when I performed in Professor Frittelli's Master Class, a monthly class where a few people would play and get critiqued so everyone could learn from it. Public shaming, the great pedagogical tool, right? Answer:

No. I felt strange and isolated from everyone as it was, so in my brain, "*Master Class*" was emblazoned as:

MASTER CLASS!!!

I had no practical concept of my skills in relation to the other students. I was raised in such a vacuum, I could only gauge myself against recordings of famous dead people. In comparison to the greatest dead violinist in the world, Jascha Heifetz, I was horrible, so my preparatory mantra became, *Please don't listen. Seriously, don't. Oh God, they're going to listen, aren't they?!*

I've always thought it's harder to perform in front of five of your friends than five hundred strangers, and this was a perfect example. It was a small room, everyone stared at me as I got up to play, I took twenty times too long to tune my instrument, nodded to the pianist to start, and proceeded to have a panic attack that melted my brain stem into pudding.

I don't remember much. Actually, I remember nothing good, just every single mistake. Out of about five thousand notes, probably four dozen were fumbled or out of tune, but instead of brushing it off, each mistake stabbed into my psyche. I imagined the inner monologue of the other students watching. *Look at the weirdo homeschooled kid, she's not so great now, let's have a party and SHUN her later!*

I got to the end of the concerto. I bowed. There seemed to be five hours of mocking silence (probably three seconds without mocking, at most). Then I looked my teacher in the eye, said "I'm sorry," burst into tears, and ran out of the room.

Well, I can't say it was the *worst* thing for the upstart, standoffish little prodigy to do, because everyone realized I wasn't as badass as I acted. After the meltdown, people were a lot nicer to me!

I eventually found my place in the school as the little overachieving sister everyone protected. "Keep Austin Weird" is the motto of the town, and it was the perfect place for me. I never wore matching socks on principle; I had a red sweater that eventually disintegrated from overuse. (Think Linus and his little blue blanket, that was my Big Dog maroon hobo sweater.) And over time I made friends. Because they talked to me, and I decided to talk back to them. Moral of the story: Mortify yourself—when you are at your lowest, you feel ironically self-confident!

I became part of the local classical music scene, on and off campus, playing wedding gigs every weekend and joining the Austin Symphony as the youngest member in their history (until a cellist named Doug joined, who was two months younger. What an ass). I lived at the music building for almost five straight years, practicing twelve hours a day, rehearsing from the time I arrived until they locked the doors at 11:00 p.m. Every single night.

And I loved every intense minute of it.

Oh, and that other full-time degree I was getting at the same time? Yeah, that was happening. But it was mostly just advanced theoretic mathematics, so how stressful could adding THAT on top of everything else be? Psh.

[Ego Math Stuff]

I'll be honest: I got my math degree mostly for my dad and grandpa, not for myself. I never longed to become a calculus professor or dazzle the world with my elite accounting skills. I enjoyed it, sure. I liked being different, and I especially liked working hard at something and getting an A in it. That was the thing I REALLY liked. Getting good grades. It was pathological. At campus gatherings I'd introduce myself as, "Felicia Day. I have a 4.0." Not EVEN kidding.

For any math student, the two hardest classes were the ones you took at the end of your degree: Group Theory, and Real Analysis. They were legendary. I knew people who could kick Stephen Hawking in the mind nuts who'd failed out of the classes twice. (A ridiculous exaggeration, but it seemed like a cool sentence.) But I was feeling pretty cocky about completing my degree and sticking the 4.0 landing. My dad promised me $200 if I made it, so there was a natural incentive for me to obsessively study with no breaks for four years straight.

I decided to take Group Theory over the summer, which was a shorter semester and even MORE risky than usual, but hey, I was the golden 4.0 child! Nothing could bring me down. Except colossal arrogant hubris, right?

I'm not gonna try to explain Group Theory in any specificity, but it's the most high-level theoretical math you can do at an undergrad level, analyzing abstract algebraic structures and how they recur throughout mathematics, like rings, fields, vector spaces . . . okay, I've lost you. And myself. I couldn't remember one bit of it if you waterboarded me. (Patched together that description above from Wikipedia.)

There were maybe fifteen students in the class, and it was taught by a guy who tutored me a bit before college, call him Dr. Cleary (yes, I had math tutors growing up, like royalty). During his first lecture, I was lost. Completely and utterly lost. It was like the professor was speaking a dead language, but it wasn't nearly as cool as Klingon or Elvish.

This was gonna be bad.

First test came around, I'd studied a LOT, and I got . . . a 23. Yes, out of 100. A TWENTY-THREE. This was my next-to-last semester. I'd maintained a 4.0 the whole time. A red-marked *23* on a test was not just devastating for me, it was . . . well, yes. It was devastating. That's a good word to use. I almost threw up, but I was in the back of the classroom crying really hard, and I had a weird suspicion that if I did both at once I'd have an aneurysm, so I just concentrated on weeping softly without drawing attention to myself.

After class, I went up to Dr. Cleary, holding back the tears and vomit. "Um, so, uh, what can I do to get an A in the class? Is it impossible now? Should I drop it?"

Dr. Cleary had ear hair like a werewolf, but he was compassionate. Unlike a real werewolf would be. "No, you shouldn't drop it, Felicia. You take it, and if you fail, take it again. That's what a lot of people do."

"I can't do that! I have a 4.0!" It wasn't sinking in through his ear pelt: 4.0 was the DEFINITION of "college Felicia." Didn't he get it?!

He said, with an earnest comb-over and a voice way too calm for the situation, "You know the best thing that could happen? Get a B in this class. Life would be so much easier for you after that. It's not a big deal."

Old Felicia, looking back on young Felicia, nods wisely. She says to herself, "That's the best advice I've ever heard. Why do I care about my GPA so much? Why do I have to be the best at everything? Does it really matter if I have ONE B?"

But young perky-tits Felicia can't hear her thirtysomething, wrinkled self. She is determined to get an A, no matter what Dr. Clear-face said. She will break herself doing it, oh yes she will! Muhahahahah . . . hah.

Ha!

I went to every single office hour for Dr. Cleary for the rest of the semester. I went to OTHER professors' office hours and pretended to be in their classes to get extra help. I went to one of my mentor professors, Dr. Davis, who had nothing to do with Group Theory at all, but I thought she might be able to get Dr. Cleary to go easy on me. All she said was, "He's right. Get a B, it will be fine." Psh. I did NOT get her a Presidents' Day gift that year.

I took over the physics lounge at the math building for the rest of the summer to study. I checked out dozens of textbooks. I studied math as hard as I ever did the violin, six, eight hours a day. When I hit a wall studying alone, I looked around the classroom and recruited a study partner, a guy named Jesse, at random. "YOU! I'm cute. You got a thirty-eight on the test. Get in here, we're studying all summer!"

Jesse was a gawky but loveable guy with a huge Adam's apple and feet the size of small canoes, and was my constant companion in my quest to master this devil subject. He was at my side all summer, whether he liked it or not, eating frozen burritos for every meal and drinking fifteen cups of coffee a day. Every step of the way. Except when he left for a week because of stupid KIDNEY STONES. What a slacker.

When the final test came around, I'd soaked myself in so much Group Theory that I was seeing numbers fly all over peoples' faces, like in *Good Will Hunting* or that Russell Crowe movie where he was super smart and then went crazy for an Oscar. I was ready. There were five questions on the test, and as I scanned the final, I saw that I knew *every one of them* by heart. I looked up, smiled a "Screw you, Dr. Cleary!" smile aimed at the area on his skull where his comb-over met his ear hair, and got to work.

When I got the test back the following week, it had a "100" at the top in red marker.

And a *frowny face* next to the number.

Yes, a FROWNY FACE. *My teacher wanted me to get a B!* But I didn't give him the satisfaction. I spent a summer of my life dedicated to something I'd never use again. *I showed him!*

One semester later I did, indeed, graduate with a 4.0. I had done it. And after that, my GPA did . . .

Nothing. I never planned on going to graduate school. I wasn't applying for jobs that used grades as a measurement. I didn't need that GPA for any single reason other than to SAY I had it and impress people.

I could turn this into an argument for "Let's reward a high GPA after college in LIFE! Can we get priority seating on Southwest? A free monthly refill at Starbucks? SOMETHING to make four years of my life chasing this arbitrary number WORTH it?!" (Great idea. Never gonna happen.) Or I could argue that if I'd been easier on myself and gotten 10 percent worse grades I could have had 50 percent more friendships and fun.

If someone's takeaway from this story is "Felicia Day said don't study!," I'll punch you in the face. But I AM saying don't chase perfection for perfection's sake, or for anyone else's sake at all. If you strive for something, make sure it's for the right reasons. And if you fail, that will be a better lesson for you than any success you'll ever have. Because you learn a lot from screwing up.

Being perfect . . . not so much.

Oh, and make sure if you're working hard at something it's in a subject you ACTUALLY want to remember something about ten years later. Because I'm reading the rest of this Wikipedia entry, and this Group Theory stuff is INCOMPREHENSIBLE.

[Dating? Nah.]

This section will be pretty short, because there's not a lot to talk about in these areas, haha . . . I'm serious.

You'd think a girl whose mom drove her to college every day wouldn't exactly have a hoppin' collegiate social life. And you would be correct. I didn't get invited to parties or date anyone for most of those years, because I was underage and for some reason, everyone was afraid of the whole "statutory rape" thing. When I turned eighteen, there was a small party on the fifth floor of the music building, because the guys could flirt openly with me and not get arrested, but even then, I was too shy to hook up with them. Not that I didn't have the desire to. In my heart, I wanted to be with one of the classical guitarists because they were the biggest pick-up artists in the musical world. They had the quietest instruments, which meant they could play in the hallways and not get yelled at, so they sat around playing sexy classical guitar all day, and panties just DROPPED. But the few times one started circling me seriously, my professor would see us together and say, "That flamenco scam artist? He's not good enough for you, get back to work." And I'd skitter off back into my practice room and lock the door against a potentially glorious and rhythmically complicated seduction. Sigh.

On a basic level, I had no idea how to approach men. My general strategy was to stare at them from afar, with big Margaret Keane eyes, waiting for them to come over and save me, like a quirky indie film ingénue. Let's be real: that character makes for good film festival fodder, but no one wants to take on that damage in real life. Manic Pixie Dream Meh, more like it.

The only guy I dated for any significant time in college was able to crack the awkward ice because of a toilet flush. In "Carmina Burana," specifically, a piece we played in symphony together. He was a percussionist, and it's a totally dramatic piece, overwrought in the most entertaining way. You'll recognize the main theme from every shirtless warrior movie, but in one of the sections there's a percussion instrument that LITERALLY sounds like a toilet flush. Every time we'd play that section, I'd look back at this cute blond percussionist with two earrings in one ear and start snickering as he played that instrument, whatever it was called officially. Unofficially, it was "that toilet flush thing."

One day after rehearsal, he approached me in the elevator and said, "Funny about that toilet sound, huh? Do you wanna go to lunch?" I was nineteen by then, I'd figured out I didn't have to get married after one date, and said, "Sure!"

We had a great time together because, surprise! Turned out he loved computers as much as I did. He collected Atari consoles (ALL of them, he had over fifty on shelves around his bed) and we'd go to his apartment and play Kaboom! and Tank instead of fooling around. I guess to some people that might have been weird, but I got my rocks off watching someone be amazing at Duck Hunt. Whatever.

My percussionist boyfriend graduated and went away to grad school a few semesters later, but not before he introduced me to the most amazing thing I'd ever experienced. No, not sex (I'm a lady; I don't write about that) but something just as good: the World Wide Web.

It was just emerging as a THING in the mid-'90s. Boggles the mind, but Friendster and MySpace weren't just punch lines to jokes at one point. One day I was trying to find a reference book for a term paper at the library, and my boyfriend said to me, "You should use the computer lab, way easier than the card system." Of course, I thought he was an idiot. I was a library loyalist, paper was always superior, and flipping through the index cards made me feel industrious. But I went into the computer lab and, lo and behold, on the desktop of the music lab computer was a thing called a "browser icon." I was confused.

"*Mosaic*? What's that?"

I double-clicked and stared at a blank university database search page. There was a search bar in the middle with no instructions, no guide. That was it. Not user-friendly, even for a prototech native like me. I called over to the guy who worked there, "Hey. How do I use this browser thing?"

He said, "Go to AltaVista dot-com and just search for stuff."

"Do I spell out the dot?"

"No, it's a period. 'www.altavista.com.' "

"Sorry. Can you type it in for me?"

He, rolling his eyes, marched over and typed on my computer. I was about to get uppity and say, "Um, you don't have to be condescending . . ." but as soon as I saw what appeared on the screen, I flipped out and forgot to be defensive and angry.

"OH MY GOD. I CAN SEARCH FOR ANYTHING BY TYPING IN THE BOX?"

"Um, why are you yelling?"

"Sorry, dude."

It was like my childhood dial-up technology but better. A place with unlimited messaging, no expenses, *I could type to other people with a keyboard for free about anything I wanted! This browser was . . . and then it had . . . and I could . . . what?!?!?!?*

My world was *transformed.*

After completely forgetting about whatever stupid scholastic thing led me there, it took me about two hours to plant my flag on the internet and create a personal university home page with cutting-edge green bubble GeoCities-like background art that I designed all by myself. Here's the actual picture of my stunning artistry:

Amazing design. Perfect layout. (Font: default New Berolina. Oh, yeah.) True story, I ended up earning a spot on a "Babes of the World Wide Web" directory with this page. It was a disgusting and skuzzy website that compiled the URLs of the "hottest women on the internet." And I made their top fifty list in 1998, yeah! If you blow up my head shot, you can clearly see the faint outlines of a mustache on my upper lip. In the early internet days, standards were definitely lower.

Before I left the lab, I made Condescending Guy show me how to dial up to this "internet" thing from my house using a program called Telnet, and after that I never looked back. Or searched for a social life for the rest of college. With this kind of technology, who needed it?!

Between my web browser, math degree, playing violin and video games, and never ever dating anybody, I had the most comprehensive, unsocial college experience in the history of man. But still, I loved it. I loved being on campus. And learning. And getting perfect grades. And being the little prodigy everyone took care of. I occasionally went to kung fu movie screenings at the college rec center on Friday nights (yes, my mom went with), and I prided myself on knowing every out-of-the-way single-stall restroom hidden in the obscure campus buildings, like Archaeology, where I could poop in private. After four years I graduated as the valedictorian of my class and delivered an overly earnest speech on "Finding the Art in Your Science." The whole time I was lucky enough to find work as a musician, so everyone assumed I would continue on to graduate school and have a great violin career, and all the expectations were heaped and heaped and heaped.

After graduating, I didn't do anything with any of it.

Um, why?

There was a student in Mr. Frittelli's class, I'll call him Carl, who was from New York City and a "BRO!" personified. With an accent like a construction worker and hands like ham hocks, he was the most out-of-place guy you can imagine in the classical music world. And he wanted to play the violin more than anything else in his life.

Thing was, Carl was not good. He didn't start early enough, he didn't work hard enough, he sometimes brandished his instrument like a weapon. No one thought he could make a career of it. But he WANTED it so badly. You could see it in his eyes when he watched other people play who were better than him. It broke my heart.

All I wanted was to give Carl my abilities. Even though I had been devoted to music for so many years, I knew deep down that I didn't want to play violin for the rest of my life.

I admire the crap out of Carl now, because he was doing something he loved more than anything. And he was determined to do it, regardless of how successful he was. Carl played the violin because he had a PASSION for it, and screw the rest of the world. Even if he had to get a day job that wasn't musical after college, and was only able to pick the instrument up at night before bed, to play ONLY for himself, it made him complete to have that in his life. And I think every minute he spent playing that violin was a moment he was spending his time right.

I wanted to find something like that for myself. I had a sense that I hadn't found it yet, that there was MORE out there somewhere. I knew I wasn't complete by playing Pachelbel's Canon for the five hundredth time at a wedding. I knew I wouldn't be satisfied by teaching adorable toddler robots "Twinkle Twinkle Little Star," either. I wanted to find a dream that I couldn't live without pursuing. Regardless if I made it or not. Just like for Carl, the "trying" of it would be worth it.

So after graduation, I moved to Los Angeles to become an actor. That was what my heart told me I needed to TRY to become. I knew I could do it.

After all, I had two Real Degrees. How could I fail?

4

Hollywood:
Not a Meritocracy?

> My adorably naïve history as an actor and why, in my mind, I was destined to "make it" in Hollywood based on several community theatre chorus girl parts.

For some reason I always knew I wanted to be an actor. I think it was because I read too many fantasy novels as a kid. There was always this nebulous feeling of destiny, like I was the *Chosen One*, foretold to vanquish auditions for *One Life to Live* and *Hannah Montana* with talent bestowed by the gods. In my heart I was certain: The sword of stardom would be mine!

81

My aunt Kate was the one who got me hooked on performing. She was the coolest person I'd met by the age of preschool, and that's pretty frickin' cool. With big permed '80s hair, she drove a yellow Datsun fastback and let me ride in the front without a child's seat. The sound track to *Cats* was permanently stuck in the tape deck, and we'd sing "Memory" at the top of our lungs when we'd sneak out after bedtime to get curly fries at Hardee's. Together, at the ages of six and twenty-four, we were practically Thelma and Louise.

Aunt Kate had briefly moved to New York City to become a musical theatre performer after college but was forced to return home because of health reasons (type 1 diabetes, the worst). She got a job as a librarian but kept acting locally, because no matter how many times you have to sing "Somewhere Over the Rainbow" for bored senior citizens at an Alabama dinner theatre, once performing is in your blood, you can't get it out.

She also introduced me to the concept of a "work ethic" nineteenth-century-early. Aunt Kate developed horrible cataracts because of her disease, and for a summer became partially blind. She needed several surgeries to fix her sight but couldn't afford to stop her job. She had to keep her health insurance. So, as a seven-year-old, I was recruited to go in every day and basically do her job with her. Shelving. Scanning in books. Chiding people: *"Mrs. Bertram, you have to return that new Danielle Steel. Someone else has been waiting for it for weeks!"* The best part is that her tiny branch was located *inside* the local mall (must have been a weird Alabama phenomenon), so she paid me for my time in items from the Hello Kitty store across the way. A Little Twin Stars pencil case was my first legitimate wage payment.

No job since has left me feeling so well rewarded.

When my aunt found out that a local Huntsville theatre group was staging *To Kill a Mockingbird*, she decided that I was absolutely perfect for the lead part of Scout. Mainly because my haircut matched the kid's in the movie (through no fault of my own; again, my mom made bad choices).

"If you wear overalls to this audition, Felicia, you can become a star!"

I won't lie. "Star" sounded super appealing to my seven-year-old self. If I couldn't be reborn a princess, this sounded like the next best thing.

There was only one catch. "The audition paper says ages ten and above, Aunt Kate."

"If they ask, just tell them you're ten."

"But that's a lie."

"You want them to hire you to be someone you're not. So if you lie well, you're showing them how great you're gonna be at the job!"

I thought about it for a few beats and couldn't argue with her logic. It was pretty confusing. So the next day I lied and got the part! It was a great lesson to learn so young: Never let the truth stop you from getting what you want.

Rehearsals started up, and I loved every minute of it. Not the work of acting necessarily, that was all right, but the feeling of becoming part of "The Theatre." (Say it with a British accent, that's how I wrote it.) No matter your age or race or background, all actors are treated pretty much equal, which is heady stuff for a seven-year-old: "equality." I found out that being treated like I was important fit me like a glove!

The kid who played my older brother in the play, Jackson, was not so taken by my adorableness. He was thirteen and despised me because he didn't like my upstaging him with my dazzling performance. (At least that was what my aunt told me.) I was great at memorizing my lines AND his lines and never hesitated to yell out when he flubbed them. I couldn't understand why he was so sensitive about it! After all, he was the old one who should have better neural connections; I was only SEVEN. (Revealing that at rehearsal one day was quite the hat trick. Everyone was impressed. Except Jackson. He hated me for that, too.)

During one dress rehearsal, he screamed "Shut up!" when I helped him out with his dialogue ("You forgot the 'eats raw squirrels' line again, Jackson, jeez!"), and after that incident, the line was drawn, Hatfields and McCoys–style. Our families started sitting on the opposite sides of the auditorium, and we referred to his mom as "Old Fat Thighs." The atmosphere got tense.

It all caught up to me during our first matinee performance. There's a section in the play where Jackson's character says, "Run, Scout, run!" and he pushes me to get away from the scary Boo Radley dude who turns out to be . . . well, it's only been fifty years, no spoilers. Anyway, this almost adult (in Arkansas) kid pushed me SO HARD that I flew eight feet across the stage, tripped, and hit my head.

THUMP!

The audience gasped. Time slowed. As I staggered up, I remember noticing how everyone was leaning forward in their seats. It was suddenly very exciting to be an actor.

"Is she hurt?" "Was it part of the play?" the crowd murmured as I stood there, stunned. My aunt had told me a true thespian never breaks character. So I decided to use the moment like Meryl Streep: I burst into tears and ran offstage yelling, "MOMMY!"

The screaming match between my mom and his after the show would rival any sweeps-winning episode of *Dance Moms*. Carnations and Chips Ahoy! were used as projectile weapons in the greenroom. The fight went on so long that eventually I started feeling guilty. Because Jackson looked so miserable sitting on the opposite side of the room and . . . okay, I'll admit it. He was cute and I had a crush on him.

WHATEVER, YOU GUYS!

Nothing got friendlier between us after that, but he never shoved me like an MMA fighter again, and I never corrected him on his lines again. (Even though he DID mess them up. A lot.) For years after that play, my family would tell the tale of how "That kid Jackson tried to murder Felicia," and we were pretty convinced he was going to grow up to be a serial killer. I recently looked him up on Facebook. He became a dentist, so same difference.

Here's the awesome irony, though. A local newspaper critic attended that specific matinee performance. Afterwards, we got an amazing review that singled out the "fantastic physical performance of the young actress playing Scout." I even got an award that season! So basically, what I learned was that I love the stage, and that it's advantageous to have slightly older men physically assault me. (Just KIDDING! Gawd.)

I'm sure my aunt would have mentored me through many a great role after that, helping me conquer the Northern Alabama theatre scene with my glorious skills, but it was not to be. My family moved to Mississippi right after the play ended. But I'd developed a taste for the stage, and I wanted to keep doing it. I couldn't let go of the idea that I was pretty amazing.

Confidence: 3
Self-Awareness: 0

We moved a lot during my childhood because of my dad's medical training, but whenever we'd arrive in a new city, I'd immediately search the *Pennysaver* or community center bulletin boards for auditions. Of any kind. And no matter what little backwater town we landed in, people were putting on a show! Usually a revival of *Oliver!* (I was in that play four times as an orphan. I also played a prostitute twice in *Sweet Charity* before the age of fourteen.) Sometimes the productions were *very* small, like an 8x8 space behind someone's garage, or at an old folks' home where the star was an eighty-five-year-old with Alzheimer's, but as long as they accepted me, I joined up. I couldn't help it. Like tuberculosis, once you catch it, the need to perform is always inside of you.

Unfortunately, when you're the "new kid," you don't get the juicy roles right away. There's usually a seniority system, and sometimes I was passed over for a speaking part by someone who wasn't great, which was disappointing to me but enraging to my mother.

"They only picked her because she was Jewish!"

Well, Mom, I was auditioning for Anne Frank in *The Diary of Anne Frank* at the Louisville Jewish Recreation Center. I think maybe there were justifications.

As I mentioned before, my mother never had the follow-through to be a true stage mom, but she was supportive in pushing my performance career in strange and arbitrary directions. Around twelve, she signed me up for singing lessons with a woman named "Miss Hilda" who led a church choir and looked like she'd been a spinster since the late 1890s. The woman wore dickies with her sweat suits.

Miss Hilda taught me German art songs, which is SUPER useful when you're auditioning for *Tannhäuser*, but if you're trying to rock a solo from the Who's *Tommy*, not so much. My mom couldn't tell the difference. Singing was singing, and her daughter was amazing at it, therefore everyone must listen! She became alert for opportunities for me to shine with my newfound skill, on stage and beyond.

One day we got in the car and started driving to Ohio. Randomly. My brother and I were confused.

"Where are we going?"

My mom had a copy of the newspaper in her lap and thrust it at me. "They're rebooting *The Mickey Mouse Club* and searching for new talent! You're auditioning!"

Panic. "But I don't have a song prepared!"

"Just do that one Miss Hilda taught you last week!"

"Um . . . really?"

"Either that or 'Happy Birthday.' You have such a beautiful voice, it won't matter, you're a shoo-in, baby!"

I wrapped my mom's faith around myself like a straightjacket as we drove three and a half hours to a nondescript Holiday Inn in Cincinnati. I marched into the run-down ballroom with a number 239 pinned to my shirt and, when prompted, began singing Schubert's "Gretchen am Spinnrade" for the touring Disney audition committee.

"Meine Ruh' ist hin
Mein Herz ist schwer,
Ich finde, ich finde sie nimmer . . ."

"THANK YOU!"

And that was the closest to becoming a Disney kid I ever got. Thank goodness.

Several years later, we were living in San Antonio, and my mother met a man whose daughter took ballet class with me. Of course, the conversation turned to my *fantastic* singing voice, and it turned out that the guy knew a guy who had a brother who recorded music and made albums. In his garage. Talk about kismet!

Except he didn't do pop music (or German lieder), he specialized in Tejano music. The accordion music that the Tex-Mex region adores. Objectively, it is very danceable.

To most humans, I would not be the FIRST person you'd pick for stardom in this particular field. For one, I didn't speak Spanish, and two, there was that *really* Caucasian thing going on with my face. At this point I was a bit older, fifteen, and I strongly registered my objections, but when my mom saw an opportunity, she couldn't let it escape.

"Your voice is so pretty! That girl Selena is popular, and you're just as pretty as her! You can do this!" There was no arguing. I would be her Central Texan Eliza Doolittle.

My mom immediately bought language tapes to play in the car. "*Mi casa, su casa . . .*" everywhere we drove, I drilled. I started flamenco class, which had nothing to do with Tejano but was similar enough to tap dancing that I enjoyed it, and after a few weeks of intense training, we met with the recording guy to talk debut album concepts.

Now, this guy should have been rightfully laughing us out of the state, but my mom is somehow able to make the most insane ideas seem plausible. At least when you're in her sphere of contact. Once she's gone, you start to catch yourself, like, *Hey, now. Wait a second . . .*

We sat there in a tiny recording studio behind a nail salon, and my mom painted the headline "White Tejano Star Takes San Antonio by Storm!" with such vivid enthusiasm that the producer dude, slurping from a two-hundred-ounce sweet tea cup, was totally digging it.

They brainstormed as I sat there silently, praying for an earthquake or tornado to kill us all. I kid you not: the strategy was to change my name to "Felicia Diaz." Which was pretty considerate, because I got to keep my first name, just add the accent, like "Feliz Navidad." I don't know why I was so uptight about it; the plan screamed success!

The two of them came up with tons of debut song concepts, mostly with the word *corazón* in them (my violin playing was a HUGE asset, special skillz, y'all!), and we left planning to come back the next week to start recording.

In a very sad way, fate intervened. Before we could get into breaking the lyrics down phonetically for me to learn so I could insult millions of people and their culture in MP3 format, the superstar Selena was murdered by a fan. The whole future of Tejano looked to be a bit iffy. I was able to get that violin scholarship to go to college during the confusion, and my future of becoming a superstar disappeared into the mist.

Lo siento, mi amor.

[Hollywood, I'm Inside You!]

Because everyone discouraged me from getting a degree in theatre (thank you, everyone), I did the math-music thing in college, but in the back of my mind I was always going to move to Hollywood and become an actor. I could analyze my motivations until the day I die, but there just wasn't any logic to it. I never had a doubt that it was how my life was going to go, and I was going to make it happen. My mother was often impractical, but she did instill a "leap and look later" attitude that's pretty much responsible for my whole career.

Days after I got my Real Degree, I moved west. I didn't go completely unprepared (I was only 95 percent stupid at the time), I had a few cards up my sleeve. I'd saved up a lot of money by living at home and playing violin professionally and having my mom drive me to college for four years, so that torture paid off in the end. I had also volunteered at tons of film festivals in Austin and made connections with "Hollywood insiders." Most of them were screenwriters, which

I later found out are the most useless connections you can have (only LA valets get treated worse than LA writers), but my friends did help me figure out where to live, how not to get killed on the freeways, and what kind of acting head shots immediately went into the trash. My first photo is NOT an example of what they suggested was successful.

Maybe it was my obsession with Clark Gable and Carole Lombard's

relationship coming into play, but for my first LA photo shoot I decided to go for the "Look as old as you can at age twenty-one in an Ann Taylor silk blouse" strategy. Ultimately, in my mind, the pictures didn't matter. Because I was still wrapped in that blind, unerring faith: Felicia Day was one audition away from a *Vanity Fair* cover, no matter what.

You see, I was raised on the great American girl dream. Talent and experience don't matter. If you're pretty enough, you'll be discovered while sitting at an outdoor table in Los Angeles, plucked out of obscurity and placed onto magazine covers by a producer randomly driving down Sunset Boulevard in his Land Rover who pulls over, yanks a cigar out of his mouth, and yells, "You! Get in the car! I'm making you a star!"

Strangely, no matter how many cups of coffee I've ordered at outdoor cafés on Sunset Boulevard, this has never happened to me. I did, however, make one of the most inauspicious filmic debuts of any actor ever, so that's something I can brag about.

There's a weekly paper called *Backstage* where producers post notices to find unpaid and/or nonunion actors to audition for their terrible-quality stuff. Mostly student films in black and white with no sound included. As a newbie actor, applying for these projects is the best way to get experience, because no one with any résumé credits whatsoever would stoop low enough to do the work. You send out hundreds of head shots and get maybe one audition out of the bunch. And each response makes you feel like, *This is my big break! I'm on my way to a party in the Hollywood Hills, watching Johnny Depp undress to get into a hot tub. Better shave my legs!*

From one of my first submission batches, I got called in to audition for a movie in a building that was located on Hollywood Boulevard. After living in LA for over a decade, I now know it's the sleaziest place in town to have a meeting, but at the time I was like, *Damn, girl. You made it already!*

The role was for an "Untitled" horror film. (Really, how hard is it to come up with a name? Just pick one and change it later, guys.) I arrived at the address to find a dozen girls sitting on the floor in the hallway waiting outside. No chairs.

One after another, the actresses went into the room, read the lines, and then proceeded to SCREAM at the top of their lungs.

"AAAAAAAAH!"

Sometimes there was a pause, muffled discussion, then a second take.

"AhhhhAHHHH AH! Ahhhhh!"

The casting director, a kid who looked like he was a high school intern from Omaha, would escort the actresses in and out, shuffling through cute girls like a deck of cards. "Next!"

The whole process made me nervous. I'd never screamed on cue before, so I practiced a few silent ones with my mouth closed while I waited, like a cat coughing up a hair ball.

"Mmmmm! MmmMMMmm! MmmmM?"

Eventually, channeling Miss Hilda's vocal training in the back of my mind, I convinced myself that I could nail this situation, no problem.

When it was my turn, I got escorted inside the office and saw that it wasn't really an office at all, more of a closet. There were actual brooms hung up behind the door.

The director sat in the middle of the tiny room with a tripod and camera next to him. He was wearing a dirty T-shirt and dark wrap-around sunglasses. The room had no windows, so the shades thing seemed excessive, but it was Hollywood. I assumed important people looked douchey.

"Okay, okay, stand there . . ." He had a French accent and waved me into the middle of the room. The Omaha "casting director" squeezed in to read with me. With no preamble, the director started the camera and crossed his arms.

"Go." Huh? Oh, that was his version of "Action"? Right.

I performed the scene.

I was adequate.

"Good good." A long pause. "So, what I feel strongly for this character is we will have a shower scene, yes?"

I was confused. "A what?"

"A scene. In shower. To show character. Are you comfortable with shower scene?"

"Uh . . . you mean naked?"

He made a minimizing gesture. "Just breasts."

Okay, well, HOLD ON! I'd prepared myself for something like this before my move. I'd heard about casting couches and naked switcheroos and Hollywood tainting and corrupting innocent girls' souls, and I'd vowed to myself and my dad, "I'll make it in Hollywood, but I'll make it clean!" I would never show my breasts. Except for Scorsese, or Spielberg, or two dozen other exceptions. But no, Sir Wraparound Shades, no! You will not have my boobs.

I gathered myself proudly. "No, I don't think so."

"Will be beautiful, very artistic. Only to learn about character . . ."

"No, thank you." I could tell he was less interested.

"Okay, scream."

I screamed. It was a good scream. A silent "thank you" to my probably-dead-by-then singing teacher Miss Hilda.

"Thank you. Go."

And I left, head high, knowing that I'd dodged a bullet. I would NOT be working for that exploit-y French guy, ever!

Except I did. I was hired the next day to be the non-boob-showing friend of the lead girl in the ultimately titled *Serial Killers*.

Of course, I took the job. But I wore very unattractive underwear to the set, just in case they were trying to trick me with infrared cameras or something.

The movie was shot in houses all over Reseda, a porn suburb of LA, and I found out later that the director primarily made soft-core cinema to pay the bills, so that added up. *Serial Killers* was his attempt at breaking into more "artsy" content. But still with lots of titties.

I worked three days on the movie, knowing the whole time that the girl I was acting opposite was eventually gonna show her boobs in a "character shower" scene, and I treated her with a touch of pity. We never talked again afterward.

Despite the rough experience, I was paid $90.00 in the form of a check for five days' work, and I was thrilled. I had MADE MONEY acting just two months after moving to Los Angeles! This whole crazy leap of faith was really gonna work out for me!

The day after I went to the bank, I got a call.

The check had bounced.

I called the film production number, but everything had shut down and disappeared, and in the end, I never got paid. Yes, the first dollar I'd ever made acting never existed.

I was mildly upset, then cheered myself up by spending $150 of my paltry savings on an ornate, rococo gold frame. I hung the framed check in my office so that I could one day relay the story to James Lipton on *Inside the Actors Studio*. A perfect representation of my ignoble first job in Hollywood. I was sure ol' James would eat the story up.

I limped from tiny project to tiny project after that, but there were no more bounced checks. (Good thing: I didn't have the framing budget.) The next few years were incredibly slow and frustrating, but I never thought about giving up on acting. Coming from the academic world, I had faith that whatever the obstacle, I could push myself further and harder than anyone else and I would eventually win.

Oh, you naïve, cute child.

Between the long "no jobs in sight" stretches, I concentrated on what I could control myself and attacked the task of "Let's be the best actor ever!" with as much pluck and adorable gusto as I did learning mathematical Group Theory. (Which I had completely forgotten the minute I graduated. But people were super impressed in auditions when I said, "I have a math degree," so: semi-worth it.) I took acting classes everywhere I could. The one I recall most was with a guy whose name I will change to Grant, because he was the embodiment of a human turd.

Grant was about five feet tall and had a very large head, which is supposedly good for TV acting. Large heads, not shortness. I guess he pegged me as a problem when I first entered class. I was too fresh and friendly and looked like I needed to be psychologically assaulted? Something like that.

Whenever I asked a question or had a comment in class, Grant would act like I was an idiot. "Of course, it's not like Pinter. Did you actually READ the plays?" If I performed a scene, he would tell me I was terrible in a pretty straightforward "Felicia, that was terrible" sort of way. I remember he once said, "You aren't good at comedy, don't even try. Concentrate on being a victim, it's a better casting for you."

I couldn't understand what the problem was. I was *always* the teacher's pet, it was my *specialty*. What was WRONG with this guy? Missing an opportunity with an A+++ suck-up here, hello!

I didn't realize that there are places in Hollywood that prey on impressionable young people, aiming to break them down in order to build them up again. Run away from any teacher whose biggest acting credit is "Banker" in a Lifetime movie of the week? No, I was new to town, I figured since this person had purchased advertising in the back of a trade magazine saying that they were an acting teacher, it was my problem! The fault was obviously with me and my crappy abilities.

The last straw was when I performed *Breakfast at Tiffany's* in class. It was the scene where Audrey Hepburn goes upstairs to George Peppard's room and sings "Moon River." I thought because of my beautiful singing voice, I would finally get a compliment out of big-head Grant. But at the start of the scene, the actor playing opposite me came out from backstage, said his first line, and he was . . . STARK NAKED. Like, his junk was all out and dangling like a turkey head.

Never rehearsed, never discussed with me. And . . . yeah. I was a bit thrown.

"Keep in the scene, Felicia, my God, be an actor!" Grant's huge mouth flapped at me from the sidelines like Terrance and Phillip from *South Park*.

I kept saying my lines, but it was very hard to keep the warble out of my voice with the other actor's bait and tackle hanging out. I stumbled through the scene, shrinking in anticipation of what the teacher would say to me afterwards.

We sat on the stage for evaluation. Grant turned to my scene partner first. "Nick, that was fabulous, so brave. You really went there. Everyone applaud Nick." Everyone applauded. Then Grant turned to me. "Why are you here? You were given an opportunity to use Nick's gift to you and you ruined it. Audrey Hepburn would be ashamed."

Well, I'm pretty sure Audrey Hepburn wouldn't want to see her scene partner's dick hanging out for no apparent reason—she was pretty classy—but I wasn't sassy enough at the time to say that, and I broke down crying.

"Where was THIS in the scene? Dismissed." Annnnd class was over.

I went home, my self-confidence crushed.

And I kept going back for another month.

Yes, I was a total idiot, but there was a weird, cultlike atmosphere in the class, and I had recently moved out of my mom's house and didn't know any better. Every day Grant's assistants told us if we quit, we'd never make it in Hollywood. They used that old cliché line AND I BOUGHT IT. Clearly, they were right; I mean, the girl who told me that had two whole lines on *Will & Grace*!

I finally wised up after a more experienced actor told me, "You probably shouldn't be paying three hundred dollars a month to go home crying every night," and I decided Grant wasn't gonna teach me to be good by abusing me OR being nice to me. I called up to quit class.

His assistant heard me out, then said, "You can't quit."

"Yes, I can. I just did."

"No, you have to have an exit interview; it's in the class rules. Come down and talk to Grant tonight."

"Come down tonight to talk?" I was holding my then boyfriend's hand because I was so scared to confront these people and looked over. He shook his head vigorously.

"No, I don't want to do that." My voice trembled. Lame.

"Do you want to work in this town as an actor?"

"Yes."

"Well you better . . ."

STOP, FELICIA! It's a trick! RUN! "No. Wait. Good-bye!"

I hung up, and they immediately called back. Again and again. All afternoon, and later that week. I didn't have to cancel my phone number because they stopped calling, eventually. But I'm not going to lie. I weighed it as an option.

That wasn't the ONLY bad situation I encountered taking classes around LA, but it was definitely the worst. Anyone can put a sign up and call themselves a teacher. Hell, one time I went to an audition class INSIDE a laundromat. But after the Grant thing, I learned that the most important thing about taking classes is to find a place *you look forward* to going to. That way you actually get better at what you love and don't want to retire and become a barista every time you walk out the door.

Also if you want to start a new profession, it's better to get some references on your instructors and not pick them out of the back of the classifieds section.

[I Need a Job, Please!]

Education mastered (slightly), I decided I needed to conquer the other side of Hollywood: the business of getting work. Specifically, I needed acting work to pay my bills. And to get acting work, you need an agent. To get an agent, you need to prove you have worked as an actor. It's like a set of Russian nesting dolls, stabbing each other from the inside with tiny needles.

For a year after I moved to LA, I searched for someone to represent me. That's a great process, because it makes you want to shoot yourself. The few agencies that would meet with me gave me amazingly blunt and contradictory opinions.

"Fix your teeth so you don't look like a rabbit."

"Your smile is charming, your best asset!"

"Lose some weight, and you could be a lead."

"Gain weight; you're too bony."

"The red hair isn't working, make it darker. No one likes a ginger."

"Love the hair, very unique. But pad your bra. It's very flat up there."

(No one contradicted that last piece of advice.)

My favorite was, "You're pretty, but you could use a . . . *shoop*, you know?" The agent made a gesture down his nose with two of his fingers, accompanied by a slurping sound. I think he meant a nose job. I also think he was an asshole.

It was hard to hear all the criticism, but I was still relatively fresh off the boat and naïvely self-confident, so I spurned it all. I knew by being myself, I had achieved some awesome things in life. Like local theatre awards and two Real Degrees. I was studying hard, I was doing all the right hard-work things, I was a unique and precious unicorn and FINE exactly the way I was!

Also, I couldn't afford a nose job. I would just have to work hard to make up for the ugly face.

After my five millionth interview, I got an agent who didn't want to rebuild me from scratch, and I started auditioning for television commercials, which was great, in a metaphysically soul-searing kind of way.

As a commercial actor, you get sent out on appointments several times a day with no preparation. Just audition over and over for the opportunity to become a human prop. A prop in a car ordering do-nuts, a prop being startled by a Transformer, a prop eating limited-release KFC panini sandwiches over and over until the prop pukes . . . I've done it all.

I have a great "love to please you!" attitude and look good in polo shirts, so over the next several years of my career, I did amaz-ingly well in this area. If you are persistent enough, you can make a hell of a good living and work only two days a year doing television commercials. Half my nose snuck on camera for an Old Navy com-mercial during the 2004 Olympics, and I made more money than I'd ever made in my whole life. And the variety is fun, if you can remove yourself as an actual FEELING PERSON from the process.

On different projects I got to skydive, play with parrots, and eat five bags of Cheetos in an hour (FYI, it isn't how I suspected. If you eat enough Cheetos you will NOT actually poop an extra-large Cheeto).

I got hired to walk down a street thinking a whole monologue of silent thoughts about weight loss while drinking liquid yogurt. Later, they asked me to audition to be that same monologue voice in the commercial. *Which I ended up LOSING OUT to someone else.* Yeah, I lost a job to be my **own inner voice**. Strange, because I sound exactly like my own voice in my OWN HEAD when I think about liquid yogurt. But I got paid extremely well, so the empty feeling of being treated like a puppet was fine? Sort of?

Actually, not.

Acting in commercials was never my life goal. I wanted to be on TV or in an indie film with Parker Posey about quirky people having family issues around inheritances. Or Parkinson's. SOMETHING where I wasn't being yelled at for wrinkling my prop shirt or squeezing the prop burger too hard so the prop mustard started oozing out the back.

After five years of acting and making a great living, I started to forget why I moved to LA in the first place. And so did my family back home.

"We saw you on that post office ad, you're so cute, are they going to turn that into a TV show?"

"That's not how that works, Mom."

"Well, here's an idea. You should be on that *NCIS* thing with Mark Harmon. You grew up on military bases, you know that world!"

"Gee, you're right! Why didn't I think of calling them before? They've probably been waiting by the phone for YEARS!" Le sigh.

On a renewed quest for opportunity (i.e., last-gasp attempt to fan the dying fire of my dreams), I hustled to get hired on bigger projects. I finally accepted that my dazzling 4.0 GPA wasn't the trump card in this new world that I'd thought it would be, so I started making changes. And I did them out of desperation, which is always a first step into the mouth of existential doom.

I cut off all my hair when an agent suggested it. And, for some reason, I started getting hired more. "People like you looking less like a lead character and more of a 'best friend'!" Cool! I loved listening to prettier people complain about their relationships, I could work with that!

During one audition, a casting director said I looked "adorable" in a dorky rainbow scarf, so I started dressing only in bright, colorful clothes. Like a hot first-grade teacher who says, "My quilted cardigan hides sensible cotton lingerie under here. Come undress me, but first, please use a coaster for your drink."

The makeover cherry topper was when I got nerdy librarian glasses. They made me look older, but in a weird, accessible way. Suddenly I could play late thirties as a twenty-seven-year-old. More work flooded in. Good change! Good Felicia! Yay?

And after switching up all the superficial stuff, I was the same person underneath, but for some reason, people *couldn't stop hiring me.* The snowballing feedback made me abandon the whole "What does Felicia want to be?" and I started doing whatever anyone told me they wanted from me in order to succeed. Lo and behold, it WORKED!

I got tons more commercials. I overcame my nuclear-meltdown nervousness in auditions to get a few jobs as recurring characters on TV shows. I didn't work every day, but for the average actor, I started to have a career I could brag about at cocktail parties. With my head-to-toe makeover, I'd found my niche: cat-owning, stalker-y secretary.

And I played the same part again and again and again.

SO ACCESSIBLE!
SO QUIRKY!

Thing is, the "cat secretary" role was never the focal point of any scenes. She was a decorative character, adding a touch of flavor to offices across the TV landscape. Most of my lines were in the vein of "Mr. Garrett, your wife is on line two. Can I go home early to feed my fifteen animals, please?" Either that or I was hired to do laundry. I've washed laundry in a half dozen different TV shows. I guess I look clean? Which is kind of a compliment . . .

But who was I to complain? Every show needed secretaries! Finally, after six years of struggling in Hollywood, I was finding bigger success. My grandma got to see me on an actual TV show and brag about it to the checkout clerk at Kmart. I had pinpointed a salable stereotype I could play for the next twenty years, living the nomadic life of audition after audition (accompanied by panic attack after panic attack), begging to answer fictional phone calls in innocuous ways for decades to come . . . and I hated it.

The role was a shadow of the kind of characters I wanted to portray. No one had a place for my geeky, weird, homeschooled, video-game-loving inner self. They could only see me as an extremely clean but neurotic secretary. "Your nose is too weird to be the focus of the show, but you're perfect for answering the phone in the background in a quirky fashion!"

I painted myself into a tiny corner, so I could be simpler and cleaner and more hirable by Hollywood. I was rewarded for it, but it made me miserable, and I didn't even realize it.

When the system you want to be a part of so badly turns you into someone you're unhappy with and you lose sight of yourself, is it worth it? Er . . . probably not. But self-reflection wasn't my strong suit at the time. I just knew that I kept getting opportunities I couldn't turn down, that I would have killed to have in the dry years before. I never stopped to wonder, *Why am I so depressed all the time after all this success?*

Instead of making big-girl decisions about my future, like setting goals for myself, working on other characters I could play, or hell, signing up for some good ol' therapy, I turned to another world.

An online world. A game called World of Warcraft.

5

Quirky Addiction = Still an Addiction

How my obsessive personality steered me into a twelve-hour-a-day gaming addiction and an alt-life as a level 60 warlock named Codex.

Anal retentiveness is one of my most attractive genetic traits. (I also hit the genome lottery for "The ability to pack a suitcase efficiently.") As a little kid, I filled out index cards on every movie I watched and stuck them in a yellow recipe box. The cards were filled with critical insight and searing analyses. Par exemple:

National Velvet

4 Stars

This made me cry because horses were in it, but the girl had purple eyes. I want purple eyes too.

I tend to obsess over things easily. Like eating oatmeal every morning for a year, wearing a pair of sneakers over and over again until my big toe pokes out, and having an unhealthy fixation on the martial arts personality Jean-Claude Van Damme. (Did you know his real last name is Van Varenberg?) When I travel, I read dozens of books about the locations I'm visiting, to the detriment of SEEING anything. I can't show you many pictures of my trips to Thailand or Vienna, but if you want to discuss the history of Buddhism or secessionist furniture design, I'm ready to dish!

I have been borderline-ready to become addicted to something my whole life. And more common addictions got ruled out because I'm weird. Alcohol, I metabolize too fast (two sips I'm twerking, five sips I'm snoozing). I'm too neurotic to do drugs because they give you meth teeth (not *all*, but enough to make me concerned), and sex addicts get vagina warts. Or so I read on the side of a bus. What's left that could become a trigger area?

Video games, of course.

At the height of my "auditioning for burger commercials" acting career in late 2005, my brother, Ryon, invited me to join a new online game called World of Warcraft. For nongeeks (Are there any of you out there reading? I like your hair!), it's a "Massively Multiplayer Online Role-Playing Game" where millions of people can play together simultaneously. Ryon had been playing for a few months with his friends and thought I would enjoy it.

My brother and I hadn't been close growing up. I know that sounds weird. You'd think, two kids locked in a house together, there should be some great indie-film, Wes Anderson bonding happening, right? Not so much.

I could maybe trace it back to when he was three or four years old, when he ate chocolate ice cream in the messiest way possible, spreading it all over his face, and I'd dry heave and scream, "Mom! Tell Ryon to eat neater!" and then he'd smear it even BIGGER, right up to his eyebrows. Or it might be the time when he was ten, when I wanted to watch a miniseries about Anastasia, the maybe-not-murdered Russian princess, on our only TV. *He* wanted to watch Monster Truck Racing. My mom wasn't home to arbitrate, so he forced me to try to strangle him with a phone cord.

Either of those incidents could have been what separated us emotionally. I'll talk to a therapist about it and get back to you. We loved gaming together, but that was about it. We kind of just EXISTED with each other. I regret that, because if we'd supported each other more, I think we could have been more secure in our respective weirdness when we finally encountered the real world (which was WAY later than it should have been because we were homeschooled). The fact he was reaching out to me to play an online video game together was flattering. I jumped at the chance.

BUT A TINY CAUTIOUS LITTLE JUMP.

Because I didn't know much about this Warcraft thing, but I did know that anything online with other people in a "game form" could be potentially hazardous to my time-health. The previous year, I'd developed a slight addiction to another online game called Puzzle Pirates. It was brilliant in its design, AND you got to customize your character, *who was a pirate*. In all categories, it was a four-hour-a-day winner.

My Online Pirate Sublet

The tasks in the game were simple but fun puzzles. There was a carpentry puzzle (like Tetris), there was a sailing puzzle (a variation on Tetris), and about three other puzzles with . . . Tetris-like qualities.

There were overall goals, too. The better you played, the faster your ship ran. The faster your ship ran, the more stuff you gathered. The more stuff you gathered, the more money you earned. The more money you earned, the cuter the outfit you could buy, and the cuter the outfit . . . well, that was a basic end goal. The outfits.

I was KILLER at running my pirate ship, particularly with the navigation (quasi-Tetris-like) puzzle. I mean, savant level, guys. And after a few months of playing, I impressed enough people to make a lot of in-game friends, and we banded together to form a regular "crew." It became the people, not the clothes, that kept me logging online day after day as we sailed the virtual seas.

Both of my closest friends in the game were stay-at-home moms. "Ploppyteets" had just had her first baby, and you could tell from her attitude, she did NOT know what she was getting into with the whole "Shoving a human out of the bio-oven." She'd type things like, "Sorry, have to leave. This baby wants to rip my tits off all day." I never figured out much about her personal life, but I pictured her in a trailer park in Nevada, breast-feeding as she solved puzzles and smoked cigarettes, ashes dripping on the infant's forehead.

The other mom we'll call "LadyLee." She had a newborn and a two-year-old, and her husband traveled a lot. LadyLee seemed like the kind of woman who was pretty and sweet but unhappy in her marriage. She had gained a ton of weight after her last child and was depressed all the time, so she didn't leave the house. Ever. Real American Dream story. Instead of worrying about herself, LadyLee would counsel people in the crew about their love lives, their schoolwork, anything they needed, all through the game's chat interface. She was always there and sweetly comforting, like an AI big sister.

There was one incident where I got a job on *Days of Our Lives*, and afterwards, the producer called my manager up and said, "We will never hire this girl again." I had exactly five words in the episode, and I couldn't figure out how I screwed them up so badly. I kept having panic attacks in my sleep, reliving the single line, "My princess, how are you?" over and over in my head, as if somehow it could un-ruin my career. LadyLee was the only person in my life who could get me to laugh about how stupid the whole thing was.

"Oh, was that the scene with Sami? She had an affair with her brother-in-law Tom, and then he murdered his own brother, which caused her to be committed to a mental hospital and meet another woman who was MARRIED to Tom, and then they broke out together and got revenge on Tom by ruining his shipping business. They probably didn't like your nose."

Then LadyLee bought me a new Pirate hat in-game, which had a feather in it and REALLY looked good with my character's hair design, and suddenly I was weeping onto the keyboard, typing, "Thank u, life saver. <3."

She was a yar pirate friend. So it was sad when things went off the rails SO BADLY for her.

A new guy, "TreeMaster," joined the crew a few months in, and he and LadyLee started chatting with each other privately. A LOT. I'd load cannons (in a PINBALL Tetris-like game) and gossip with Ploppyteets about the Lee-Tree relationship.

"Are they on her ship together in *private chat* again?!"

"Uh-huh. Wow, my kid is a crap fountain, how do you plug them up? There's no manual with this thing."

Things escalated, LadyLee and TreeMaster bought a ship together (hello, virtual commitment!), and I could sense something was going too far between them. I tried to caution her.

"You and TreeMaster are hanging out a lot, is that a good idea, Lee?"

"Oh, Howard and I just like working together, that's all."

I stopped typing in shock. HOWARD? They'd advanced to real names?! This was serious!

But LadyLee seemed so much happier after she met TreeMaster (as much as you can glean emotion from alphabetical letters placed together in a chat interface), and I felt bad about being negative. LadyLee was an adult, she had things under control. Plus, their ship was SO FAST, who was I to judge if they worked that well together?

An acting job took me out of town for two weeks, and when I returned to the game, everything in the crew had collapsed. The only person I could track down online was Ploppyteets. I typed to her, frantic.

"Where is everyone?!"

"New Mead Brewing mini-game just got released. I'm balls at it."

"Um, ok. Where's LadyLee and the crew?"

"She dissolved the group. Won't be online anymore :("

"Why not?!"

"She left her husband last week for TreeMaster, he found stuff between them on her computer, and I guess she's losing custody of her kids. She hasn't logged on since we talked last week."

"WHAT?!" Because of sailing the pixelated seas, this woman's whole life had collapsed? "Are you kidding?"

"I wish. Bonus, my baby has a thing called 'colic.' I'm looking to trade her in for a Chevy if you know any takers."

That was the last day I ever played Puzzle Pirates. I was worried about LadyLee and felt incredibly sorry for her but had no way to contact her outside the game. I didn't even know her real name. It felt helpless to care about people I'd never meet, who could disappear on a dime. I would miss Ploppy, too (even though I worried about the future of her offspring), but it was too hard to play anymore.

It had gotten too real.

GOODBYE DYSFUNCTIONAL SOCIAL SITUATION!!!

That eight-month "Yo-ho-ho!" sideline made me aware of my personal slippery slope in the online gaming area. It was VERY slippery. But I rationalized that my brother was reaching out to "bond" with this new MMORPG game, and that was something I couldn't turn down. And if something went wrong, at least I knew how to reach him via phone to say, "Don't leave your husband and children for a random guy named Howard who's really good at virtual carpentry!"

I bought World of Warcraft in the summer of 2005, right after I lost a part in a television pilot to a girl who looked EXACTLY LIKE ME. Red hair, pale lumpy face, if you squinted at our head shots we looked identical. And it was depressing. To come in second choice to . . . myself? So I installed the game and created my first character, named? You guessed it. Codex.

In this game, people group themselves in private "guilds" instead of "crews." My brother was a member of a guild of players called Solaflex, and it was for "little people" only, which sounds offensive, but the fact that everyone had to be a gnome or a dwarf character was funny at the time. Because they're all short. Other players who were not gnomes or dwarves were tall. So in-game, when you ran around together, it was a tinier group of people than average.

You had to be there.

I created a Rogue (Thief) character, because I enjoy channeling my inner kleptomaniac, and stepped into a world so real, so "graphically advanced," that as I hopped around in the starting area, clutching my little beginner dagger, I fell in love. Deeply. Unutterably. In love. This probably sounds strange to nongamers. I understand. The best analogy I can make to real life is this:

You know how sometimes you go to another city and, while driving around, you see a house that looks so cute and inviting that you fantasize about what it would be like to drop everything in your life and just move there? Like, you see a cottage while on vacation in Belize, and think, *Prices are dirt cheap, people look chill, let's DO THIS!* It's a feeling of new possibility. Of starting fresh. Imagine capturing a kernel of that in your own life *right now*, by sitting at your computer and paying $15.00 a month in subscription fees.

That's what it's like to bury yourself in a virtual world.

And it WAS a completely new world. With hundreds of players running around, animals attacking you, different categories of chat rooms, tons of buttons and commands, at first, I was lost. Every two minutes I'd type to my brother for help.

"Which buttons move me?"

"Where is my backpack screen with my clothes in it?"

"What is 'leveling' and how does it work?"

"I'm stuck in a wall, can you come get me?"

All these questions are the real-life equivalent of, "What is this thing at the end of my arm, and how do I close it around items to lift them?"

After giving me a brief, thirty-minute crash course of the logistical life of being a gnome, Ryon went to play with his fancy level 60 friends and left me in the baby starting area alone, an innocent level 1, to be killed over and over by virtual spiders and boars. (Classic sibling behavior.)

Thinking back on that introductory experience, I can never blame anyone for saying, "I don't get video games, they're too intimidating." They can be. VERY. And unfortunately, chances are that an anonymous teen gamer on the other side of your monitor will respond to appeals for help with, "It's easy. Get with it or get out, asscrack." There's no easy way of getting into the hobby even if you WANT in, so a lot of people, especially girls, give up. The learning curve is too steep to climb.

But don't worry. I climbed it. The hard way.

Over the next months, I played a few hours a day, but TERRIBLY. I didn't know I had special skills to kill things faster, so I did the basic "STAB" attack over and over. It took upwards of two minutes to kill each creature. It should have taken ten seconds. And I died a lot. It was not fun. I got frustrated and finally typed to my brother.

"Sorry, but I think I'm done with the game. It's too hard."

"What? Twelve-year-olds play this game, what's too hard about it?"

"It takes too long to kill things. My mouse finger hurts."

"Did you not level your talent tree? Are you using Sinister Strike followed by Eviscerate?"

"YOU'RE SPEAKING GNOMISH TO ME!!! I'M MAD AT YOU! HELP ME PLAY PLEASE!"

"Okay. Fine. God."

That night we started brand-new characters together. Gnomes again, of course. My new character was named Keeblerette, and I put tall, white, penile-inspired hair on her. Something I regretted instantly. It was not, at the time, reversible.

Ryon created a warrior girl named Mochi with pink Princess Leia buns, and we were ready to rock the virtual world together!

We advanced our characters to the max level after about two months of playing. We played and played and played, a few hours every night, and I used all the right buttons my brother taught me, and it was awesome. Chatting with each other in the game was so fun, like texting while driving. Except not dangerous and illegal.

"Let's go to the swamp area."

"No, let's do the undead area first! Watch me blow up this slime monster!"

"Wow, so much goo. Dance in it!"

No dungeon could defeat us, no monster best us. Actually, that's not true, we died about five million times each, but we were stronger together than on our own. (*After school speciaaaal!*)

All the exuberance and sense of purpose rubbed off on my real life. I started walking around feeling . . . happy. A casting director was rude to me, and I thought, *Gosh, she probably had a bad day*, rather than dry-heave sobbing in the car afterward. A part of Hollywood-defeated Felicia Day was "fixed" by my double life as a tiny little penis-haired gnome. Getting the opportunity to know Ryon as an adult through playing the game together was a huge part of that. And why I fell in love with the game so much. It felt empowering to prioritize our time together, rather than living at the beck and call of acting appointments. Even if it was just, "Let's kill that skeleton boss tonight!," it felt like I belonged somewhere with him. Finally.

Before you say, "Wow, this chick is on a nerd plane of existence I can't relate to" <slams her into a locker>, the thing about a computer game character is that a part of you BECOMES that character in an alternative world. That little gnome Keeblerette was an emotional projection of myself. A creature/person who was more powerful, more organized and living in a world where there were exact parameters to becoming successful. "Kill forty wyverns, get points that make you stronger. Check!"

When we graduate from childhood into adulthood, we're thrown into this confusing, Cthulhu-like miasma of life, filled with social and career problems, all with branching choices and no correct answers. Sometimes gaming feels like going back to that simple kid world. Real-life Felicia wasn't getting more successful, but I could channel my frustration into making Keeblerette an A-list celebrity warlock, thank you very much!

During those hours of playing, I befriended a lot of the other members of my brother's guild, just like with my old pirate crew. And even though they could all theoretically disappear on a dime, it was comforting to start up the computer after a day of feeling like an idiot because I had to pretend to drive a car by steering with a fake prop steering wheel, extolling the "Amazing Honda handling!" at a commercial audition. It felt like I could endure any lack of fulfillment in my career as long as I knew my "friends" were online to play with when I got home.

> 6/7 16:51:26.790 Keeblerette has come online.
>
> 6/7 16:52:18.553 YoMamaz: Oh yeah, new helm timez!
>
> 6/7 16:52:27.803 YoMamaz: Hey Keeb!
>
> 6/7 16:52:41.752 Mochi: Yo Keeb.
>
> 6/7 16:52:57.504 Spitball: Keeb wassup?!
>
> 6/7 16:53:01.110 Spitball: Finally we can get some fun started!

It was like *Cheers*. But where absolutely no one knew your name.

[My Professionally Destructive Gaming Career]

The big move in my/Keeblerette's virtual life was about six months after I started playing. My guild decided to advance to a more complicated part of the game, which moved me from gaming hobbyist to full-time addicted employee of World of Warcraft.

The game has especially challenging areas that require getting large groups together called "raids." In the early days when I played, these events required forty people logged online AT ONCE for up to *eight to ten hours* at a time. Clearly, the programmers didn't have enough real-life social relations, or that basic design concept would never have occurred to them.

It was a nightmare. Have you ever thrown a party and tried to get EXACTLY three dozen *specifically qualified* people to attend? Even if they RSVP, half of them never show up, right? And if enough people don't show up, you can't throw the party. So you have to recruit random people at the last minute who you've never met before to fill up the roster. And *they* turn out to be greedy eleven-year-olds from Estonia, who you're FORCED to keep around in order to limp through the evening's festivities, and . . . yeah. Just typing all that out gave me stress flashbacks.

After attempting it a few times, our guild decided it was too small to attempt one of these fancy raids alone, and we joined forces with a slightly bigger guild named Saints of Fire. These guys took their gaming SERIOUSLY. In order to participate, everyone was required to install voice chat software so the leaders could coordinate everyone's actions verbally during the fight. Like air traffic controllers. This also meant that we would finally be able to hear one another's voices for the first time. It was a move that was . . . socially terrifying.

People will finally know I'm really a girl! Half the girl characters are played by guys who PRETEND they are girls, but this is really it, they will hear me and KNOW! What will they think? Will they judge me? Most important, will I get downgraded on the warlock roster?! Anxiety almost made me log off and never log back on again. But I had to keep playing. It made me happy. So I sucked it up and bought a huge pair of gaming headphones with a mic attached to them that jutted out across my mouth and made me look like a 1-800 operator.

The first day of the combined raid, I logged into voice chat, nervous. "Hey, guys, uh, Keeb here. Checking in for warlock duties!"

There was a beat of silence, then a flood. "Oh crap, Keeb's really a girl?!"

"Yeah, I told you so!"

"Really? I owe you a hundred gold, SacBallzsky."

"I'm good for it."

"Hey, Keeb!" "Hi, Keeb!" "Good to hear you, Keeb." "Nice voice!"

There was a flurry of excitement, but no one seemed to get THAT worked up about my vagina-dom, thank goodness. I've heard from a lot of other women that revealing their gender online sometimes invites reactions of "BOOOOONER! Let me throw sexual innuendos at you until you fall for my hot elf self!" But our raid turned out to be more female friendly than that. Probably because the Saints of Fire leader was a girl who could verbally rip your dick off.

Her name was Autumna. I mean, that was her character name. (At this point let's just agree that they're indistinguishable.) Autumna sounded young, like she was in college, and had a voice like a hatchet.

"I'm docking you attendance points."

"Argue with me, you die."

"Rambo, tranq the hound! I'll cut you into pieces in your sleep if YOU DON'T WAKE UP, IDIOT!"

To expect gentleness from Autumna was to squeeze a knife and not have your fingers cut off. I loved her.

As we settled into the new gaming hierarchy, I realized that the voice chat just exaggerated what people used to be like in type. They could be outgoing, or quiet, or "people you definitely wouldn't want to hang out with unless you desperately needed them for the game."

There was one mage named Gooroo who always logged online with a loud "GOOROOOOOOOO!" When he killed things with a big magic spell, he'd yell "GOOROOOOOOOO!" Pretty much everything was accompanied by a "GOOROOOOOOOO!" He got muted a lot.

There was one druid who always had his mouth full of a meatball Subway sandwich when he talked, and a warrior who never spoke except to quote *The Big Lebowski*. I found my sweet spot in the societal hierarchy by becoming the resident DJ. I figured out how to connect my music to the voice chat program, and would spin everything from New Order to Snoop Dogg/Lion/Dogg to Lady Gaga while we prepared for fights. Our signature song was "One Night in Bangkok," a late '90's synth song about night life in Thailand, and everyone would stop and make their characters dance when it came on, singing the chorus at the top of our lungs through our headsets:

You'll find a God in every golden cloister
And if you're lucky then the God's a she.

I don't think anyone understood the lyrics. (Or we were all really liberal. Probably both.) At any rate, small things like that made raiding with forty strangers the best thing in the world.

We needed those joyous social highlights, because the game raids required a TON of coordination, not only to assemble the exact number of qualified people, but also to get your character ready for action. "I have to spend three weeks gathering equipment? You're saying I need to do *homework* to play this video game?!"

Yes. That is what they were saying.

We'd rush the same monster over and over for weeks without succeeding. "Turdburger, you let me die again! Stop eating while we're fighting, I can hear you chewing your Subway!!" It was NOT a casual hobby. We raided together about twenty hours a week, sometimes just to fail the fights again, and again, and again. Sounds incredibly annoying and not like the definition of "game," which is to "play," which in turn means to "engage in activity for enjoyment," right? So why bother going through all this grief? Bottom line (just like in Puzzle Pirates): outfits.

All the best armor and weapons were acquired in the difficult mega-group dungeons. It was the Rodeo Drive of Warcraft. When you got a piece of fancy "epic" purple equipment, your character became more powerful and looked cooler when you danced on mailboxes inside the game. It's the same reason why real-life men buy sports cars and real-life women buy handbags that cost the same as said cars. (Back then, I would have salivated over a "Tier 4 Nemesis Helm" before a Hermès Birkin bag any day of the week.)

In order to win the best stuff, you placed bids according to points you'd earned for raid attendance. Basically, minutes of your life were used as currency. (When I describe it that way, it sounds horrifying.) There were only three to four items auctioned off to the group of forty people each week, so, like debates in British Parliament, things got rough. Because avarice doesn't generally IMPROVE one's character. One time my brother Mochi got reamed because people thought he was hogging equipment, so he posted the following on the forums:

> It has come to my attention that there have been bones of contention raised about a few of my raiding bids in Blackwing Lair and in the Molten Core, specifically, with my fellow raiding warriors questioning my bidding demeanor concerning the Helm of Endless Rage, which drops off of Vaelastrasz the Corrupt in the Blackwing Lair zone, and with the Onslaught Girdle, a Ragnaros drop from the Molten Core zone.

If, on any of my future bidding, you have any questions or qualms about what I am doing, and would like me to know about your second thoughts or have any ideas/suggestions for me, I invite you to write all your thoughts on the matter in a message/email/forum post for me. Then, print it out, roll it up in a tube, and stick it up your ass.

Sincerely,

Mochi

He wasn't one of the more popular members.

I, however, was very popular. I had a charming lack of fulfillment in my life, so I was psyched to be able to work hard and study like I was in college again. "4.0 in Warlock? Sounds like a goal to me!"

But as we started working through harder and harder dungeons, more and more prep was required BEFORE the actual raid time. Making potions, gathering equipment and herbs, rearranging my in-game storage unit. Most people had day jobs or school, but what was I doing during the day? Except for the occasional "Going to audition/class/coffee-with-other-actresses," I had TONS of free time. I figured, "*Someone* needs to make those Flasks of the Titan, might as well be me!"

That is when my gaming life started tipping out of control.

I started working full-time in World of Warcraft. I'm not exaggerating. Every morning before I left the house (IF I left, which I frequently didn't), I would log online and fly around the game world, harvesting herbs across the virtual globe to make potions. This hunter/gatherer trip would take about an hour or two each day, minimum. (Yes, I spent a large portion of my time inside World of Warcraft commuting.) I invested in a very expensive office chair, for my ass comfort, because I was sitting on it most the time and it was starting to spread. But I didn't care about my booty, 'cause there was looty to be collected! (HAR! Okay, no more puns, I apologize.)

At one point I thought, *Hey, I have a few hours of my day that are NOT eaten up by gaming!*, so I created an additional character to fill those up. A burly dwarf lady named Sugarz became my "backup date" in case the raid didn't have enough priests to be able to play properly. Between the two characters, I fell into a schedule of raiding six to eight hours *every single night*.

I stopped going to acting classes. I stopped performing improv. Or doing plays. Or socializing with real-life human beings. Several times I skipped auditions because I didn't have time to prepare after staying up too late gaming the night before. I ate, slept, and lived World of Warcraft.

I guess it's pretty obvious, but it was not great on my personal life. I disappeared. My friends didn't see me for six months. My boyfriend would place a plate of food next to my mouse pad, and I wouldn't look up. I'd just shove whatever was there into my mouth until my character died, or I had to pee.

"Thanks for the food, honey!" Oh wait. He'd left the room an hour before.

It was easy to ignore how destructive my behavior was becoming because there were SO MANY other people doing the same thing I was doing online. We rationalized it for one another. At the height of my addiction in 2006, I had logged a few thousand hours in World of Warcraft. That's a solid one HUNDRED days of human life. Now I think it's depressing, but at the time it was a point of pride.

I was obsessed. I couldn't stop myself. It was not healthy. But I couldn't stop. It didn't feel like there was anything else in my life to stop for.

We all have periods of our life where we're trapped, doing something we hate, and we develop habits that have nothing to do with our long-term goals to fill the downtime. Right? I hope you identify with that idea; it's the only way I can explain becoming so emotionally invested in a video game that I would get in my car and drive around town sobbing if my internet went out. I knew it was bad. But even living with a constant *Gee, something is seriously wrong here . . .* feeling, I wasn't able to make myself STOP and get control of my life.

I'm not blaming the game; I'm blaming my lack of perspective about why I wanted to fill my days with that beautiful, repetitive world. My life was unhappy, and I covered the hurt with a subscription-based Band-Aid. I just couldn't find a good reason NOT to play so much. *Dig deeper and take steps to become happier in the long term? Nah, there are monsters to kill. Worry about real life later!*

Ultimately, mistakes can be more valuable than victories. Yes,

I could have learned the lesson of "Mistakes are good!" with a MONTH of gaming rather than almost two years, but I was the head flask maker. The raid DEPENDED ON MY SKILLS!

And soon after this dark period, I used all the things I learned during those dragon-hunting months of my life to create a web show called *The Guild*.

So, not a total mistake.

6

The Guild:
A Ruthless Beginning

Whereupon I mentally abuse myself into creating something due to depression, peer pressure, and hypochondria. And it turns out way less crappy than you'd think!

The Guild is a comedy web series I created in 2006 about a group of online gamers and how they interact online and offline. (Not autobiographical *at all*. Nope.) Before I made the show, my writing career consisted of one sketch comedy class, a half-finished movie script, and some creepy fan fiction I wrote as a kid. Yes, even creepier than my video game poetry. Which was pretty damned creepy.

I'd always wanted to write. But in order to try something in life, you probably have to be exposed to someone who makes you think, *Whoa. I want to be cool like them!* Everyone knows "cool" is the ultimate life motivator, for better or worse. "Tattoo around the belly button where my skin stretches a ton eventually? Let's do it!" When I was growing up, my dad read a ton of science fiction, my aunt was an actor, my brother could fart and burp loudly, and all these things I aspired to do because I felt they'd make me a more bitchin' human being. Unfortunately, no one around was like, "I'm writing a short story about unicorns who fly spaceships!" or other brilliant ideas like that, so I didn't try picking up a pen for a long time.

Even though I didn't get to practice writing as a kid, I was an expert at consuming OTHER people's writing and daydreaming about it. The first book that made me think, *I wanna get inside this character's life like a pod person* was *Anne of Green Gables*. I'd seen the miniseries on the Disney Channel (which I hated most of the time because, MAN, were girls dumb and painted pink on there), and it made me track down every single one of the books in the series and read them a dozen times over.

The books inspired me to embrace being as weird as I wanted to be. Because it worked for Anne. I mean, she was also an annoying kid who talked too much and was uppity for her station, and everyone in the books thought she was adorable! At the heart of it, Anne was a fellow redhead I could admire. She and that girl, Khrystyne Haje from *Head of the Class*. Yeah, it's superficial, but hair color identification is SUPER important. That's why I always think, *Where's the redhead one, jerks?!* when I see those rows of stupid blonde dolls in the toy aisles. (That American Doll phenomenon is super weird to adult me, but I'd have torn someone apart to get one as a kid. I bet one day they'll 3-D print them up to make literal doppelgängers. That'll be terrifying/amazing, and I'll be there to buy mine on day one! Uh . . . for my future *daughter*, of course. Ahem.)

My fandom about the *Green Gables* series was serious business. I prayed every night for my eyes to turn greener. I planned on naming my children Anne and Gilbert, which could have been awkward, seeing as they were married in the books. I put on my life's bucket list:

"Move to Canada because Prince Edward Island is certainly the most WONDROUS place on the planet."

I daydreamed about BEING Anne. Traipsing through nineteenth-century meadows, reciting Romantic poetry (Keats was my fave, because he died with such gruesome panache.) One day, I started creating my own original scenarios of Anne doing her plucky orphan thing. But I didn't want to deal with the annoying stuff from old-timey days, like sexism and polio, so I moved up the timeline and transported her into modern life as a free-spirited teen heiress. I'd imagine Anne flying to Hong Kong on her private jet, or spying on Communists while she performed gymnastics for the US Olympic Team. Or simple things, like attending a new high school where she'd enter a classroom wearing designer jeans and everyone would gasp at how pretty she was. "Her hair is so long and red. Can I be her best friend immediately?"

I started throwing in other characters from other books into my headspace, and pretty soon I'd built an imaginary town filled with stolen IP. Perry Mason was there (of course), the whole crew from the Trixie Belden children's mystery series (Anne loved to steal Trixie's boyfriend away), Lancelot and Guinevere owned the local garden store, even anthropomorphic pigs and spiders from *Charlotte's Web* were full residents with voting rights. It got so complicated I had to start tracking my world in an accounting ledger with everyone's names, addresses, and personality traits in neat little rows. ("Friendly!" "Secret lovers!" "Murderer!") My town had it all!

I'd love to say that the stories I conjured up were deep and fraught with intellectual themes, but they were not. They were straight out of *Gossip Girl*. Anne would arrive in town with a bang, and everyone would want to be friends with her. It helped that she was an orphan who'd been left billions (à la Richie Rich) and had no adult supervision. She drove a Porsche and owned a mansion with white Corinthian columns where she threw parties every night. It had an arcade AND a bowling alley. She was such a baller.

Natch, all the cute guy characters wanted to date her. Including Perry Mason and a grown-up Tom Sawyer, for some reason. Everyone referred to her as "Anne with an *e*," and if asked: "No last name. Like Cher." My utopian alternate world lasted a good six months until my mom discovered my census account ledger hidden beneath clothes in my closet.

One day I walked in on her gathering up laundry in my room. The fact that she was cleaning was shocking enough, but then . . . I saw what was in her hands. *Oh my God. My ledger!?!*

"Oh baby, is this your writing? Do you want to be a writer? We should get you lessons, let me see!" The slow-motion horror of her opening my notebook and starting to turn a page felt like ripping my own skin off with a potato peeler.

"MOM! That's mine, stop!" I grabbed the notebook and sprinted away, trying to find the nearest bonfire to get rid of the evidence. There wasn't one around because it was July and I was inside an actual house, so I searched for somewhere else to stash my shame.

I called out over my shoulder. "They're just math problems! Can I clean your bedroom? Wash the car? Make me your slave and be distracted, please!" I shoved my ledger under the dog bed as she rounded the living room corner, praying I'd been fast enough to dodge her eye line.

I was so embarrassed. I love my mom, but she has a habit of ignoring personal boundaries. She'd have no qualms about barging in the bathroom while I was bathing and say, "You need to shave your legs, honey, you look like a bear down there!"

Thankfully, my mom didn't have a bizarre impulse to wash the dog bed, so my notebook remained undiscovered. But her unearthing of my alt world shut down all enthusiasm I had for the project.

And in retrospect it was probably for the best, because I was starting to add TV characters to the ledger at that point. Joey Gladstone from *Full House* and Anne had gotten involved in a caper with a chambermaid that was . . . it was just becoming odder as I got older, even by my authorial standards. The next morning I got up at the crack of dawn, grabbed the ledger, and dumped it into the trash can. As I closed the lid, I said good-bye to Anne. "Have fun in Cabo with Jason Bourne! Don't worry, you'll protect him from the neo-Nazis with your Krav Maga. I imagined it, so it definitely happened."

[Let's Try That Whole "Writing" Thing Again]

Fast-forward to adulthood, when I decided to revisit the idea of writing by taking a comedy sketch class in Los Angeles. Motivation? I was bored, and that's what Hollywood actors do. Take classes. And have coffee with other actors to complain about their agents.

It's a hard life.

I enrolled at the ACME Comedy Theatre in 2005 with a dozen other people who, I was sure, were 5,000 percent better writers than me. The year before, I'd started writing a screenplay because the "original screenplay" Oscar acceptance speech that year had been stirring and made me think, *I could do that!* (The speech, not the screenplay.) But the results of my work were, er . . . semi-mortifying.

Amendment: No "semi" about it. The script was mortifying.

I wrote about a girl named "Harper Jessamyn" who was graduating from college music school and couldn't decide what to do with her life.

```
                HARPER JESSAMYN
I can't help being good at the flute,
but it's a trap. What do I do, who do I
become? Cut off my fingers and cast me
in the ocean! Maybe it's better if I feed
the earth with my flesh. At least I'll be
contributing to the world somehow! There
would at least be some kind of . . .
     (BEAT)
. . . MEANING!
Harper runs away from Jax, into a prac-
tice room, sobbing.
```

Yes, there was a sexy jazz trombone player love interest, and his name was "Jax." The script included four montages of Harper Jessamyn gazing off into the sun to the sound track of Schoenberg. And then one to Bach. In the first thirty pages. Who knows what other genius montages could have been born if I'd plowed through and finished the script, but I didn't. I bailed. Ninety pages was too daunting. But writing a three-page sketch where I could wear a funny wig and make boner jokes? That was something I might be able to channel my creativity into!

The teacher at ACME, Kim Evey, was a tiny Asian lady in her thirties who had the gentle spirit of a baby panda bear. No matter how bad someone's sketch was, she would find something positive to say.

"Sure, you fell off the stage, but it was great kinetic energy!" A good teacher is someone you're willing to share your ugliest, roughest work with and who doesn't make you feel ashamed or stupid. Kim did that for me, and I loved her for it.

I wrote about a dozen sketches in the class, and surprise! My best ones were based on my (many) real-life insecurities. There was an awkward one about running into a hairdresser I'd ditched, an awkward one about my inner dialogue during a massage (I'm always paranoid about farting); "awkward" was a strong theme for me. My favorite was about a boy and girl arguing in a car about the morality of peeing in a McDonald's without buying anything.

Jill: But if I use the bathroom without buying something, it's stealing!

Robert: One flush is not equivalent to armed robbery.

Jill: Fine! I'll be right back.

Jill grabs her purse and reaches for the door.

Robert: Why are you taking your purse?

Jill: I need it . . . for feminine things.

Robert: You're going to buy something, aren't you?

Jill: No, I'm not . . .

Jill tries to get out. Robert grabs her purse.

Robert: Give me the purse.

Jill: Stop it, Robert!

Robert: You're not going to buy something.

Jill: Just one apple pie; I didn't have dessert!

Robert: Be a man! Or grow another valve!

Jill: I don't know what that means!

(For the record, I still will not pee somewhere without at least buying a dip cone.)

I wasn't the best writer in class, but I wasn't the worst, and I enjoyed myself. It was . . . strangely fulfilling?

Then the class ended, and I stopped writing because I wasn't paying someone to hold me accountable anymore. I proceeded to do nothing but play World of Warcraft for the rest of the year. But my teacher, Kim, and I later reconnected at a commercial audition (for soap or cat food or cat shampoo? I can't remember. Something with a mortifying jingle) and over lunch, she invited me to participate in a new side project.

"Would you be interested in joining a support group?"

"A what?" Ugh. Sounded lame.

"I know, it sounds lame when I put it like that."

"I didn't think that at all!" Liar. "What kind of . . . group?" I couldn't bring myself to say the word *support*; it sounded dirty, like douching or something.

"Just me and a few friends. We want to meet every week and check in with each other about our goals. Career, family, long-term, short-term. Totally informal."

People? Organized talking? Oh, God. "I don't think so."

"Do you have any goals you haven't reached? Anything you could use a boost about?"

Sure, a million things. Thinking about them, I almost started crying. "I guess I can come once or something. If I don't fit in, you guys can uninvite me."

Kim gave me a funny look. "I don't think anyone will do that."

The next week I forced myself to wake up at seven thirty for the first time in about five years and drove to a pancake house in Los Angeles to join a "lady support group." It felt like going to my first day of college. I had a panic attack in the parking lot and almost drove back to bed, but it's LA, and everyone is forced to valet, so the dude took my car away before I could escape.

There were three other women in attendance besides me and Kim. Jane, who had an oovy groovy air like her chakras were WAY in balance; Trina, who was pretty and pleasant, the kind who screamed "perfect TV wife"; and Susan, who had big hair and laughed like a trucker. They were all in their mid- to late thirties, and I was in my midtwenties, so I was intimidated from the get-go by the mass of womanhood. I was wearing jeans I hadn't washed in a week. I had a feeling they'd left those times far behind them.

We went around the table sharing our goals. I learned that Jane wanted to be a director, and she was writing screenplays in order to make that happen. Trina and Susan were actors who wanted to work more, but Trina's bigger goal was to get pregnant. Hearing that immediately made me think, *Uterus talk? Get me outta here!* but I just nodded quietly, mimicking the others' supporting-type vibe.

I got tenser and tenser as the conversation circled around to me, because I didn't know what I was going to say. I've always felt like a failure inside if I'm not already a success. If that makes any sense.

Jane was the leader, and she was so generous and open; just being around her was like taking a Xanax. She tossed the conversation to me last. "And Felicia, what goals are you working towards?"

"Uh, acting more. And writing . . . something. A screenplay? Or . . . a pilot? Yeah, a TV pilot." I grabbed "pilot" out of the air because Jane had already said she was doing a screenplay, and it's a personal rule of mine never to order the same thing off the menu as someone else. You're a flawed human being if you think two beet salads at a table is ever acceptable.

"A TV pilot? Neat! Do you have a concept?"

"Uh . . . well . . ." Sweat popped out under my armpits. *What did I know about? What did I know about?! THINK! SAY SOMETHING, FELICIA!* "Gamers?"

They all jumped in. "That's great!" "Awesome." "How unique!" Suddenly I realized, *Hey, a gamer TV pilot is a great idea!* I put it at the top of my "goals" list. I won't lie, the sheer act of writing the words "TV pilot" down on the corner of my dirty paper napkin made everything seem possible. This group support thing was gonna work out!

By the end of the breakfast, we'd named the group Chick-In. 'Cause we were all going to "Hatch GREAT THINGS!" No, I just made that up; it wasn't our tagline, we were not that dorky. Well, kinda.

Over the next six months, the group met once a week, covering pancake houses across Southern California with hope and positive feelings. (I found out later the whole meet-up idea was inspired by the book *The Secret*, but I decided to gloss over that fact, like you do when eating nonorganic produce. It's still good fiber!) And over time, the support started to work. Everyone was getting their lives organized. Step by step.

Everyone except me.

The ladies would go around the table sharing "wins" every week.

"I finished the first act of my screenplay . . ."

"I booked a national commercial! That gets me health insurance this year!"

"Met with a new manager, he's keen to help me get more TV jobs."

"We're thinking about doing infertility treatments . . ."

Then it was my turn. "Uh, I created a Word template for our weekly to-do lists."

They stared. I babbled on. "You know, because it's nice to get organized. I used a special font and imported pretty graphics."

"Isn't that the third to-do template you've made for us this month?"

"Yeah . . . but this one perfected the format! I also wrote down some Universe Goals to motivate myself." I'd thought long and hard about them, for maybe twenty minutes the night before, and was confident about my new "self-statement."

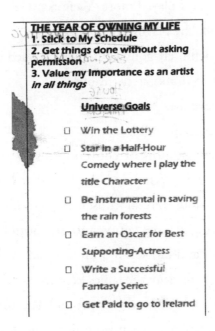

THE YEAR OF OWNING MY LIFE
1. Stick to My Schedule
2. Get things done without asking permission
3. Value my Importance as an artist in all things

Universe Goals

☐ Win the Lottery

☐ Star in a Half-Hour Comedy where I play the title Character

☐ Be Instrumental in saving the rain forests

☐ Earn an Oscar for Best Supporting-Actress

☐ Write a Successful Fantasy Series

☐ Get Paid to go to Ireland

Realistic goals all around, right? Especially the rain forest part. I was excited to hear the group's affirmation of my goals.

I got none.

Kim said, "Did you work on your pilot?"

I dug into my pancakes with a fork. Stabbing motions. "Well, I did some research." Which meant, I'd played a lot of World of Warcraft. They all sort of deflated. Because they'd heard it many times before.

The months I went to Chick-In coincided with the height of my gaming addiction. The main accomplishments I had brought in to the ladies every week were things like, "Raided Zul'Gurub. Got new armor for Keeblerette. Achieved maximum faction with the Argent Dawn . . ." I watered the vocabulary down for the civilian ladies as "Played a lot of video games," but the result was the same. I was making zero progress toward my goal of writing and acting more, and that made me depressed. So I played more. Vicious cycle.

"You did 'research' by playing video games?"

"Yeah, but I'm definitely gonna cut back." I filled the silence that followed with positive-thinking intentions.

They didn't believe me.

I didn't believe myself.

After a few more months of conversations like that, the guilt started to wear me down. That and the fact that I was gaming so much that my conscious and subconscious were bleeding together until I felt like a living gaming entity, a robot controlling the virtual character of my flesh-and-blood self. I knew I had to change SOME-THING. If only to make sure the ladies kept me on the invite list.

I went to the next Chick-In with newfound determination. "I quit the game." It was like a bomb dropped into the nonvegetarian ladies' corned beef hash.

"For real?" "Congratulations!" "That's awesome!" There was relief on their faces, like they never understood this whole "video game thing" going on with Felicia, but they knew it wasn't good. Quitting was a big step!

"Are you going to start your screenplay now?" Trina said, smiling.

She had perfect teeth. I made a mental note to ask about her dentist later, because I was flush with proactivity.

"Pilot," I corrected her. "Yeah, I'm gonna do it!" And in that moment I believed it. I could do it!

But . . . I didn't. Yes, I quit WoW cold turkey, but that didn't mean I could shake it instantaneously. An addiction isn't something you say good-bye to without pesky obsessive-compulsive strings attached.

For a month after my resolution, I stumbled through life, sleep-walking from withdrawal. Like quitting coffee times 85,000 percent. I was in a daze, itching every moment to get back online. Time became SO SLOOOOW! Like driving behind a ninety-year-old woman in a '72 Chrysler with a handicapped license plate slow. It was torture. I'd sit in my silent house, staring at the clock, the endlessly ticking clock, wondering how people endured the task of filling their whole lives with this LIVING thing. Inside I was screaming. *There's nothing to DO anymore!*

"Cold turkey" slipped into "lukewarm turkey." As a workaround, I kept up on all the blogs for the game, because that wasn't technically "playing." I followed the forums to keep up with my raid buddies, aching to rejoin them. At my lowest, I started sobbing when the game announced limited-edition pumpkin heads for people's characters to wear during Halloween and I couldn't get one. That amazing pumpkin would have covered my ugly penis hair SO PRETTY!

And all that time I was lying to my support group. I told the ladies, "Sure! I'm writing!" when I wasn't. Yes, I could have filled all those newfound minutes with actual work, but I had no confidence in myself. I was a fraud. Who was I to pick up a pen and expect anything good to come out of it? I expected perfection as soon as the pencil hit the paper, and since that's impossible, I couldn't get myself to start. Then I felt guilty about not starting, which made me want to start *even less*. And with no game to bury the feelings, I got very depressed. No wonder I didn't book any acting jobs in the last half of 2006. No one wanted to hire a clinically depressed person to sell snack foods.

Before one Chick-In meeting, I forced myself to work through some of my shame. I picked up a pencil and wrote, "Main character, played by me . . . Codex. Real name Cyd Sherman. Shy. Neurotic. Gaming addict." Then another few weeks went by, coasting on that feeling of *You did some writing! Go reward yourself!*, until it petered away into guilt again. Rinse, repeat. Despite that dismal pace, I DID get some work done on the pilot, but it took the whole fall season just to write down descriptions of the main characters. I thought, *Don't worry, Chick-In, I'll complete this thing by 2050, for sure!*

One positive thing through that agonizing, limping process was that I created the kernel of something . . . not sucky. The clichéd mantra when you start writing is, "Write what you know," so I brain-stormed all the kinds of people I'd encountered during my life of online friendships. I wrote down ideas and incidents that made me laugh and wince, and it congealed into a set of six characters (like *Friends*!) who seemed to go well together. No one was based on one person entirely (my old raid leader Autumna was the closest in the acid-tongued Asian college girl, Tinkerballa), but they all fell into categories of people from my experiences. Clara, "The Mom." Vork, "The Rules Master." Bladezz, "The Douchey Teen." Puck (later renamed Zaboo), the "Overly Enthusiastic and Doesn't Recognize Personal Boundaries" dude. Building fake people brought me snippets of joy, even though the creative process was absolute torture. And at the end, I looked at the six main characters I'd created and thought, *I want to see these people do things together!* That was in October. Annnnnnd then I stalled again. I might have started playing WoW. I'm not telling.

I didn't tell the ladies at Chick-In, either. I glossed over that part at our meetings. They seemed happy when I told them about all the fake progress I was making, so I just kept saying, "It's going great!" I didn't want to derail THEIR progress with my backwards momen-tum. I was thinking about *them* with my lies. Yeah, that's it.

Cut to December 20. I went to our last Chick-In meeting of the year. I faced the other ladies in the circular booth (Trina was finally pregnant, yay!), and I decided I had to come clean.

"I'm sorry, but I have to tell you guys something. I haven't been writing for the last two months. I've . . . been . . . playing . . . video games again." I pulled the tears back into my eyes with sheer brain-suction willpower as I admitted what a jerk I was to the supportive, no-one's-a-failure-here environment.

"We understand!" "You didn't have to lie, it's okay!" "Why did you feel the need to lie? We wouldn't have judged you!" They were all so nice about it.

Which only made it worse.

"It's just hard. I start to write something, then I look at it and think, 'This is gross and stupid,' so I stop. I can't write two words down without erasing it."

"You're great at writing sketches; think of each scene as a sketch," said Kim.

"But there are so many of them, and I don't know what happens next. I can't think of anything for the characters to do . . ." Okay, there was the breakdown. HI, TEARS! It got estrogen awkward at that point with a lot of hugging.

"You should take the holiday off. Don't write, try to enjoy yourself." Jane was so nice, like a Mother Earth priestess. But as wonderful as she and all the supportive ladies were, I left the meeting disgusted at myself. My fears had made me a liar. My friends deserved more from me. *I deserved more.*

I don't know if it was a cumulative effect of the breakfast trauma, or a mini aneurysm, but in the middle of the night something inside me snapped. I woke up at 3:54 a.m. with a full-on panic attack and a huge epiphany:

I was going to die someday. I was going to END.

And I know you can say that to yourself a million times, *Live for the now!*—I mean, it's the message of half the Ben Stiller movies ever made—but you can't understand something unless you FEEL it. Deep in your bones.

For some reason that night, I felt it.

A vivid terror gripped me. I was mortal, and I was going to die. I was twenty-eight years old. Old. Near death, in 1557 terms. Every sleep was bringing me closer to the grave, and if I didn't do something with my life RIGHT NOW, the totality of "Felicia Day" would add up to nothing.

This might sound extreme, but that voice is my day-to-day inner dialogue to myself anyway, just magnified a healthy percent. A milder version accompanies me everywhere I go. It always has. I've never been in a car accident, because on every street (especially skinny neighborhood ones) I always picture a child or animal dashing out in front of my car, trying to commit suicide on my front grill.

Anyway, as the cat started to cough up a hair ball in the next room, at 4:00 a.m. on December 21, 2006, I decided that if I didn't accomplish something huge by the end of the year, I would die a failure.

The next morning, I sat down at my computer and took a deep breath. "I will write a TV pilot before January 1. It may be the worst script ever written, but I will finish it, or . . . there isn't any 'or,' stupid girl. It will happen. This pilot will happen." And I started typing.

I would love to say that given my resolve, the muses flowed through my fingertips to produce a script of utter perfection. That once I put pressure on myself, I rose to the occasion and found joy in every bit of dialogue I gave my characters.

That is NOT the case.

Every second of writing that script felt like walking barefoot over shards of glass. I would write a bit and then I would sob, wanting desperately to erase what I'd just written. *Oh God, that's not a scene, no one acts like that. I have no idea what to make happen, who should talk next? I hate myself.* Then I would force my fingers to type more, every word feeling like I was bleeding from every orifice. I was engulfed with fear of making mistakes, of writing something stupid, of encountering story problems I couldn't think my way out of. I was, in short, terrified of the process. It was not fun.

What drove me to continue? Sheer obstinate grit.

While everyone else on the planet celebrated Christmas (except those people who don't, and that's fine, no insult intended), I wrote. A few times I made myself laugh at a joke I'd written, and then I'd get to the next scene, not know what to write next, and collapse again. Side benefit, in Codex, I was able to craft a lead character as neurotic as I was! Every fear I had about my own weakness, uncertainty about my future, and how others would judge me I poured into her reactions and dialogue. I brainstormed every funny thing that had happened to me while gaming over the years and twisted the incidents ever so slightly to fit the new world I painted. I ate nothing but takeout pizza and Doritos for days, until even my dog thought I had terrible breath.

My friends tried to get me to take breaks: "Come to the mall. Let's go to old-lady Jazzercize class. Get out of the house for a few hours!" but the awful disciplinarian in me chanted, *FAILURE, FAILURE!* and I couldn't. I was too scared to stop. (The mental abuse was overdramatic and awesome!)

I wrote every minute, up until the evening of December 31, 2006. At 7:45 p.m., I finished the first draft of my untitled sitcom script about gamers. Thirty-nine pages. And as I typed the words "The End," it was the proudest I'd ever been of myself. And I started sobbing.

My boyfriend stood in my office doorway. "Congratulations! Do you want to go out to celebrate?"

"No. I can't go out now."

"Why not?"

I sobbed, "I'm . . . too . . . happy."

I'd accomplished my goal. But I had to be ruthless with myself to see the task through. Joan Crawford–wire-hangers bad. But you know what? I don't regret letting that horrible person inside bully me at all. I finished something *for once*, and it was worth every second of suffering through that terrible, forgot-to-buy-relatives-a-present holiday season.

If ideas flow out of you easily like a chocolate fountain, bless you, and skip to the next chapter. But if you're someone like me, who longs to create but finds the process agonizing, here's my advice:

- Find a group to support you, to encourage you, to guilt you into DOING. If you can't find one, start one yourself. Random people enjoy having pancakes.
- Make a goal. Then strike down things that are distracting you from that goal, especially video games. (Unless it's this book; finish reading it and THEN start.)
- Put the fear of God into yourself. Okay, I'm not religious. Whatever spiritual ideas float your boat. Read some obituaries, watch the first fifteen minutes of *Up*, I don't care. Just scare yourself good. You have a finite number of toothpaste tubes you will ever consume while on this planet. Make the most of that clean tooth time. For yourself.

The creative process isn't easy, even for chocolate-fountain people. It's more like a wobbly, drunken journey down a very steep and scary hill, not knowing if there's a sheer cliff at the end of it all. But it's worth the journey, I promise.

I sometimes look at successful people and think, *I could do that! I could be there. I WANT to be there!*, coveting the end result without understanding the WORK that preceded it. I wanted to *have written* a script, but I had no idea how to get there. Thank goodness, I had people who encouraged me to attempt it, or I never would have been brave enough to try. I owe it all to the Chick-In ladies for their support; I needed it.

I celebrated the New Year with a script in my hand and thought, *I can't believe I did it!*

So . . . what do I do now?

TURN THE PAGE TO FIND OUT!

7

Web Series: A DIY Journey

I guess we can borrow some cameras, stand in front of them, and say the words typed in the script. Is that how this "filmmaking thing" works?

"Walk me through this slowly. People can talk to each other while they play video games?"

"Yeah. You just install separate voice chat software while you play."

I was sitting in a fancy office, looking out onto a beautiful view of the Hollywood sign. A producer sat across from me. She was a friend of a friend of someone's yoga teacher and was literally the only person I could get to meet with me about making *The Guild* as a TV show. I was pretty sure her blonde highlights cost more than my monthly car payment.

"And the characters are all playing the same game? At once?"

"It's based on World of Warcraft, a very popular online game."

She smiled and nodded. Like when you're pretending to understand something by smiling and nodding but have no clue about what the other person just said. I do that a lot about sports.

"Uh, so what did you think about my script? Did you like it?"

She looked down and started flipping through the pages. I noticed her nails were painted silver. I thought about making a Wolverine joke, but I didn't think she'd get it.

"There's so much vocabulary here I don't understand. Like, what does 'gank' mean?"

Definitely a "no" on the Wolverine joke.

"It's a gaming term that means 'kill.' "

"Can't you just say 'kill'?"

"Well, that's not authentic. I don't want gamers to think I'm a poser."

"Oh, I don't think that matters."

She laughed. I noticed her teeth were perfectly white and, through no fault of her own, she was making me feel like a peasant.

"Okay. But if I tweak that stuff, do you think my script could become a TV show?"

"Well, some of the writing shows me you're very funny . . ."

"Thank y—"

"But this is just too inside to appeal to anyone. Why don't you try to write a spec script for *The Office*? Try to get staffed on a show?"

I shifted uncomfortably. "I was hoping to do my own show. THIS show. And writers on staff don't get free dresses for awards shows. Because you know, *The Guild* would totally win awards if you made it!"

I laughed. She did not join in. She just stood up and proved to be at least a foot taller than me and had no need for Spanx under her pencil skirt. I decided I hated her.

"Well, try taking all the gaming stuff out, and let's circle back later!"

"Sure!" I realized with a sinking heart that this was it. My last chance. The project I put my soul into was never going to be made. The script would just become a check mark next to "Life To-Dos" and nothing more. As I left that room, I knew I would be leaving my dreams behind with it.

I stood and started to exit, then decided to turn back. One last time. Emboldened.

"Hey, can I get the name of your eyebrow person?"

In early 2007, after I finished rewriting my original script two dozen times, to the point where I thought, *Wow, this is absolute literary perfection!* I did the most stereotypical thing you can do with your first screenplay: I showed it to any fancy-pants person I knew, convinced they would read it and turn it into the next *Friends*. I was so confident that I started visualizing the ad campaign that would run on the sides of buses during premiere week. Me, posing with that wry, "Wow my friends are crazy, but I love 'em!" side look to the audience? You know the one.

But back then gaming was not a mainstream hobby. (Is it now? I can't tell, my head is buried so far up the anus of the culture.) And ONLINE gaming was something that especially made civilians think, *Nerd Poison!*

I couldn't believe people in show business were so uncool. The idea that it might be the reverse never crossed my mind.

Until I got rejected. A lot. Then it started to sink in.

A few weeks after my soul was shattered into a million zillion pieces (not to be overdramatic), I went to my women's support group Chick-In, and I whine-cried a lot. Afterwards, two of the members asked if they could read my script: Kim, who got me into the whole writing thing, and Jane, director and Chick-leader. I didn't see any harm in showing it to them. After all, no one else in the universe was going to see my brilliant world come to life. Ever. Sadface. With that attitude, the meeting was sure to be productive!

The three of us stayed late after the next Chick-In to discuss.

"What did you think?" I asked. Part of me didn't want to hear what they thought. I wanted to grab the scripts out of their hands and run to my car without saying good-bye.

Which wouldn't have been weird at all.

"It's amazing! I laughed out loud. These characters are a hoot!" Jane had the sweetest way of talking, and I calmed down. Compliments are like Valium to me.

Kim chimed in and agreed. "All that time you spent gaming was worth it! The characters are so real. I don't understand everything they're talking about, but . . ."

Ugh. "Of course not! No one does. All the producers I've shown the script to say it's incomprehensible." I allowed myself to be severely depressed again. That was quick.

Kim threw out the next sentence delicately, like she was fishing for a skittish trout. "I have a crazy idea. Have you thought of doing this project for the internet?"

I stared at her. "Huh?"

BACKSTORY SIDE TRIP

YouTube was created in 2005, the year I forced myself to write *The Guild*. Yes, it's weird to think that before that year, there was no YouTube. It feels like it should have ALWAYS existed, allowing us to share Taylor Swift covers with as much ease as breathing. There was Heaven, then there was Earth, then there was YouTube, right?

Shortly after it launched, Kim filmed a parody Japanese TV show short, *Gorgeous Tiny Chicken Machine*, that was as charming and odd as it sounds, and uploaded it to the service.

The video went viral, and at the time of our Chick-In meeting, she was in the middle of selling her show to a big company to make more episodes. So early. EARLY on, Kim was a planter of the first sprouts of web video. And that's why she thought the internet was the perfect place for *The Guild*.

I didn't know that, so I just stared at Kim.

"I don't understand. I thought YouTube was for kitten videos and chunky light-saber teens."

"No one gets this story who isn't in the gaming world, right? Where are the people who WILL understand it? Online."

"Huh. Good point. Gamers ARE online 24/7. I'M online 24/7."

Kim and Jane said together, "We know."

"So, uh . . . WE would make this? By ourselves?" Then it hit me, and I felt a heart-racing panic attack coming on.

For the record, I am not a risky person. If I was reincarnated from an animal, it was definitely prey. A cute one who lives in a herd, like an antelope. Or a dik-dik. What Kim was suggesting terrified me. My basic makeup did not allow me to boldly leap into self-actualization. I preferred to sit at home and complain about no one in Hollywood understanding me. That felt safer.

And Kim could sense that I was freaking out. Because I said, looking freaked out, "The idea of doing that freaks me out."

"I shot *Gorgeous Tiny* with one camera in the back of my garage. This wouldn't be much more complicated!"

Jane jumped in. "I can direct, we can split the costs three ways, it's perfect! This is what Chick-In was born to do!"

I looked at Kim and Jane for a long beat, then a strange sunrise crested through the two hemispheres of my brain. *Could it, indeed, be that simple?!* . . .

Yes, it could.

It felt like for the first time in my life, I had the power to decide something this big and make it happen. Without anyone's approval, without permission, without any external motivation like getting an A in a math class. I could do this because I WANTED to, even if it was scary and might go up in flames.

In that moment, I realized that I had been missing an amazing truth:

No matter what you feel is holding you back in life . . .

Repeat that motivational cup sentence until it gets in your gut and doesn't sound like something stupid on a Hallmark card, because it is the basis for anything that will make you happy in this world. This is something I truly believe.

I looked at Kim and Jane across the booth and nodded, feeling warm and fuzzy, like I was having the best stroke EVER. I had the power to film my script. I wasn't alone; we could do this.

We were going to MAKE SOMETHING!

[Makin' It!]

I'm going to share a dirty secret with you . . .

Actually it's not that dirty. I was trying to inject some suspense here. I'll stop.

I love crafting. Knitting, decoupage, scrapbooking, any "lady-ish" art form, I'm a fan. For about six months each. Then I shove all the supplies in a closet, alongside the skeletons of long dead New Year's resolutions, like saber fencing, playing the ukulele, and Japanese brush painting.

During my bored-actor years, I recruited lady friends to join me in doing crafting "Projects!" to relieve said boredom. (Note the exclamation mark. That was part of the vibe. Say "PROJECTS!" like a stereotypical gay character on television and you have it.) A little before Christmas and Valentine's Day, I threw parties to make holiday cards from scratch. I would buy CARTLOADS of supplies: pipe cleaners, decorative paper, gold filigree, dot matrix pictures of Bea Arthur . . . it was a bacchanal of glitter and glue sticks. I would cater tea-time foodstuffs (sandwiches without crusts and heart-shaped tarts with yuppie-berries) and serve them on flower-embossed ceramic plates.

It's strange to remember I was so vaginal at a certain point.

The same enthusiasm that motivated me to create dozens of handmade Christmas cards every year—and some for Hanukkah, because I tried to be inclusive but I didn't really understand when it was appropriate to send them to people, so I ended up shoving them in the closet—drove me to take the script I wrote for *The Guild* and turn it into a web series. From scratch. With my friends.

But through that process, I learned the hard way that making a film is not the same as throwing a Sunday afternoon tea party. It's actually . . . nothing like it at all. So I'd like to share my top five tips for anyone who decides to film a television-like show in their garage for almost no money!

[1: Befriend a Hoarder or Become One]

When Kim, Jane, and I started breaking down how we would shoot the first ten pages of my TV script for a grand total of $1,500, we realized, "Gee, we need a lot of stuff. For free. Why did I throw anything in my life away, ever?"

So while Jane pulled favors to get pro-bono crew members and

Kim worked on the icky producing logistics, I concentrated on gathering the props and superficial stuff we needed, because in my mind, being able to put together a cute outfit equaled "Fabulous at film decoration!" natch.

There was no length I wouldn't go to get the perfect object. I raided my friends' houses for props we needed, even doing the "Look over there!" trick to steal a stuffed animal from a two-year-old's hands. (She never noticed, babies are so dumb in those first few years after they're born.) Without asking, I borrowed a large, fake house plant from the set of *How I Met Your Mother* to decorate the background of one of my shots, promising my friend who was an actor on the show, "I'll have this back Monday!"

For some reason, it was incredibly important to me that each character's room be well-decorated. This was a LADY production and I was obsessed with *Trading Spaces* and other renovation shows on TV that I watched alone on Saturday nights, no WAY were any of my characters living in a hovel! Unfortunately, my exacting standards often butted up against the practicality of having no budget. "Sorry, Kim, your aunt's bedspread will NEVER do for Tink. Her palette is pinks and oranges. Let me show you the paint chips I collected from Home Depot. Can you search the old folks' home for something in this color range? No? Fine! I'll find it myself!" With zero dollars and incredibly high standards, I had to look in creative places for set decorations.

Thus began my obsession with trash.

I started trolling up and down alleys, putting anything colorful and not covered in feces into my trunk. Yes, that might sound gross and hobo-y, but it's amazing what people throw away. I found a few things, like a hot dog cookbook and a 3-D picture of Jesus, that I still have in my home. (Wiped them off with Windex, promise.)

And it wasn't only post-apocalyptic scavenging that decorated *The Guild*. I used technology to find trash, too. Since Craigslist was out of our price range, costing actual dollar amounts, I found an online service called Freecycle where people give things away, provided you immediately race to come get them. I'd click on the site dozens of times a day, like an obsessive day trader, so I could jump on a posting first.

"Broken electronics on curb near Glenoaks Ave and Hubbard St in Sylmar, come before 6pm." Perfect set dressing for Bladezz's gaming space? *BAM! GET YOUR FAST AND FURIOUS ON, FELICIA!* Sylmar was about an hour away from my house but the grainy flip phone picture of stacked microwaves and VCRs spoke to me, artistically, so I drove ninety miles an hour to beat whoever else might be vying to grab the precious treasure. Someone else could have used that DVD player for entertaining sick children, but I had a *vision* to bring to life. I *needed* that trash!

The scavenging process was satisfying, like acting out my favorite part of a video game in real life. I was smashing barrels and getting rewards! Except I didn't find gold or weapons, I found *actual garbage*. And LOVED it. Maybe too much.

The tipping point came three weeks into pre-production when I dragged home a stand-up hair dryer that was probably made in the 1960s. It was huge, dirty, and my boyfriend was at his wit's end. Justifiably so. Our place was turning into a dump.

He met me on the porch, and I could tell it was gonna be a THING. I tried to deflect with chipperness. "Hey, honey! Huge super awesome find today, huh?"

"Did you rob a salon?"

"No! I found it on the sidewalk with a 'Take Me!' sign attached. It was fate!"

"Is there a reason for this 'fate'? Like, do you have a place for it in your script?"

"No, but it screams comedy to me!"

"That's what you said about all the free yoga balls, and now my office looks like a gigantic Chuck E. Cheese." He moved closer and examined the hair dryer. "There's still hair on this thing! Don't bring it into the house. Or anything else you find on the streets. Please?"

"Fine, I'll leave it in the driveway, gawd!" What a hypochondriac.

After that, I stored trash in my car or in Kim's garage. Life compromises, sigh.

[2: "Favor" Is a Four-Letter Word]

There's merit in having the plucky attitude, "No problem is insurmountable if you're willing to be creative and bat your eyelashes a little!" (Not sexist, guys have eyelashes, too.)

The problems start when plucky morphs into desperation. "Please help me. Look how friendly I'm smiling, yet my eyes say I want to enslave you!"

Kim, Jane, and I recruited anyone we knew to help us bring *The Guild* to life. Literally anyone. Conversations like, "We need a baby. Who do we know who's bred recently?" peppered our prep meetings. Guilt, blackmail, you name it, we muscled it.

"Hey, I drove my hairdresser to the airport that one time when her uncle died. I'll call her up, she owes me!"

When we fell short on personnel, we put an ad on Craigslist for people looking for experience on film sets and said yes to anyone who didn't seem like they were a parolee.

"Here's a student from Santa Monica Community College who wants to do sound for us."

"Does he have his own equipment?"

"He might be able to bring a boom mic held together by duct tape."

"Invite him aboard!"

We ended up with a camera assistant who was a recent émigré from Hungary, and couldn't spatially place the clapboard in the actual film frame. *Her ONLY job.*

"No, Veronique, lower. LOWER! The general area the camera is pointed would be good! Ugh, close enough. Action."

The trouble is, when you're asking people to work for free, you can't be an exacting perfectionist.

"I know you're doing this as a favor, late at night and on weekends, but I hate what you did. Can you revise it fifteen times until it's perfect? Cool?"

I ended up having to use my own craft party skills to make our show logo for the opening credits after Kim's neighbor's cousin fell through in the graphic design department. *Because she was busy "going into labor."* Psh.

Yes, I used MS Paint and a mouse. No, I was not drunk.

I'll admit that some of the production problems we ran into were my fault. I am bossy and arrogant enough to think I have a "vision," so we needed a much bigger crew than an average web video warranted. Many times during filming, I'd start to cry in frustration at myself. "Why didn't I just write something that could be shot with one person and a phone camera?" Five minutes later, I'd run up to Kim. "Hey, let's fully CGI animate the opening credits! We can do motion capture like Gollum! It'll be great!"

In terms of free labor, you'd think that the actors would be the easiest to recruit. I mean, we were shooting in Los Angeles; that's like asking in Vegas, "Where can I find a glass of alcohol as tall as my torso?"

And things looked promising initially. We posted an acting listing for "The Guild. Web Series. Zero Pay. (Seriously, there's no pay for this thing.)" And got about 500 applications. *For each part.* We weren't special, that's just what happens when you put out a notice for actors in Los Angeles. Good thing I went through the process AFTER

I'd been an actor for a while, or I'd have immediately moved back to Texas to play "I Will Always Love You" on the violin at church weddings for the rest of my life.

But as we started going through the applications, not to insult my own profession or anything, we realized that releasing a "free actor" posting is like sending out a virtual birdcall, "Whackadoodle! Whackadoodle!" into the Los Angeles jungle. Ninety-eight percent of applicants were "swipe left" immediately. For instance, when you post this character description:

TINKERBALLA: early 20s, Asian. A sweet, doll-like face belies her acrid tongue.

You KIND of assume the photos submitted will be, at a minimum:

A) Asian
B) Under 30
C) Female

But when you allow just ANYONE to submit themselves, which we did, we got some, shall we say, "out of the box" head shots. Like a fifty-year-old Hawaiian man standing butt naked on a surfboard. Or a "current" head shot for a woman clearly taken back in the 1970s, accompanied by halter dress and Vaseline filter. Or a cheerful blonde who, for some unknown reason, posed with a cooking ladle.

(Oops, that was actually one of the actors we hired for a part who was amazing. Love you, Robin!)

The process gave me a lot of empathy for those on the OTHER side of the camera. For so many years as an actor, I'd enter a casting room and assume the people inside were thinking, *Wow, she's ugly. This girl's going to suck. She messed up a word on the page? AMATEUR!* But as a producer, I sat there day after day, watching dozens of people read the words I wrote aloud, and all I could think about was . . . uh, me.

Oh God, she can't pronounce the words. My script is unshootable, what was I thinking?!

That joke didn't work. We probably should change this to a video game drama. I'm in tears myself right now, should be an easy fix.

She's okay for the role. But why is her hair so much thicker than mine? I'm taking those biotin pills, do I maybe have cancer or something?

I wish I could say my experience casting *The Guild* helped me audition better myself—put the process in perspective as an artist and rid me of the burden to be perfect. But nah. I still enter every casting room and freeze up like a basket case.

Eventually we did find amazing people who looked adorable together and actually showed up on time, rounding out our cast in a totally balanced, free-costing kind of way. They were wonderful. I love them and will never say anything bad about them.

And I certainly won't EVER admit that I asked my friend Sandeep to play the character of Zaboo partially because he owned two cameras we needed for filming. Nope.

[3: Never Let a Film Crew Shoot in Your Home]

The most expensive part of filmmaking is getting locations to film in legally. That's why we "chose" to shoot everything in our own homes. (Choice had nothing to do with it, of course. I was just being cutesy with the air quotes.)

My house is painted like a clown car, with each room a different

QUIRKY! color, so we shot the majority of the show there. For three days straight. And even though it wasn't a big crew, having ten to fifteen people invade my private space was close to walking on the beach in a bikini without remembering to shave all the way on the anxiety scale. As an introverted person who likes everything around her to stay in its place and who personally likes to go to open houses with the express goal of sneaking a look into strangers' medicine cabinets, I knew that every inch of my home was destined to be violated.

A lot of the stress couldn't be avoided because we were working in such tight quarters. There's a reason regular film stages are as big as Sam's Club and not a small Los Angeles bungalow. One of the main character's locations was a shed in my yard, about six feet by six feet large, with a sign "Daddy's Doghouse" on the door. (Previous owner's touch, promise.) Shoving cameras, lights, actors, crew members, and an active bacon griddle into an area the size of a Fiat was not optimal. I mean, the crew was mostly comprised of ladies, but even then, the BO became stronger than the San Antonio Spurs' locker room.

I tried to preempt problems by making a calm announcement every morning, "This is my house, guys! Please treat it like your own!" But months after we wrapped, I was still finding Diet Coke cans stuck under my couch cushions and half-sandwiches ferreted in my towel closet. I'm sure no one DELIBERATELY tried to trash my home, but no matter how many times I'd say, "Please don't give my dog any scraps; he's gluten allergic," he would mysteriously get diarrhea. EVERY NIGHT. I won't even mention my frustration with male people not being able to hit the toilet while peeing. I couldn't enter my own bathrooms without wanting to wear a hazmat suit. We never could have completed filming without opening our homes to the crew, but to this day, I still have rings on my dining room table that I gaze at with bitterness. "I put out coasters. All the time. No one used them."

Despite the personal-boundaries issues, the set was a casual place that made it feel like we were kids playing dress-up in our homes. (Because we WERE in our own homes. Four feet away from where we slept.) That informality gave us the freedom to do things that would never happen on a professional set. Mainly because of OSHA regulations and child labor laws.

There's a scene in the first episode where the neglectful mother character, Clara, puts her newborn baby down on the floor as she's talking to the other guild members online. We needed to cut to the baby doing something hilarious while Clara was ignoring him. There were a ton of baby toys on set, but we couldn't find anything that made the scene EXTRA funny. Jane tried everything. "Give him that penguin. No, it looks too cute. What about his shoe?" Kid was saccharine adorable with any object, but I knew we needed to find something extra special to make the gamer crowd laugh. STEP IT UP, BABY! GIVE US THE FUNNY!

About ten minutes in, the baby started getting cranky, and we got to the point of "It's good enough." I hate that point. It's either perfect, or it's the worst thing ever made and everyone is an artistic failure, including myself. (Yay, emotional extremes!) I started running through my house, yelling back to the crew, "Give me two minutes, feed him, tickle him, stick a boobie in him! I'll be right back!"

After rifling through my office drawers like a madwoman, I found something perfect for the shot.

And no, it wasn't plugged in. I'm not a monster.

[4: Disaster Is Your Low-Budget Best Friend!]

The reason real television shows have hundreds of people working on them is pretty much for "disaster mitigation overhead." Also: it takes a village to make people look pretty. In our case, there were only the three of us to deal with everything that could go wrong during our shoot. And tons of things did. And bonus: I am plagued with the kind of anxiety that makes me dart my head around like a meth-addicted hamster! So . . . not the best combo.

When a light fell over outside one of the windows of my director Jane's house, it started a VERY minor brushfire. I immediately thought, *Oh God, the City of Los Angeles is going to arrest me for arson. And we don't have a permit to shoot here. We're all going to be arrested, then sued in* The People's Court. *Must scout overpasses for future homesteads on the way home tonight.*

Of course, none of that happened, but the landlord did find out about it and forbade us to shoot at that location again (forever and ever for the rest of eternity). So we all had to sneak in separately the next day to finish one last scene, with a plan that was so intricate, it could have been taken out of *Mission: Impossible.*

"Joseph: Enter back door at 10:54 a.m. Felicia: Front door at 11:07 a.m. Lana: 10:20 a.m. through garage. Carry craft service in a single grocery bag. DO NOT BE LATE!" I've never been more nervous going to someone's house in my life. I wore an outfit with a huge hat and sunglasses like Audrey Hepburn in a spy thriller. I parked half a mile away and, as I approached the house, I ran through the back door, feeling as if a sniper was outside waiting to take me down.

We finished the scene, but with me talking in a very creepy whisper. (And people ask me why my character Codex is so neurotic.)

Another time we were filming at my own house, and in the middle of the shot, the sound guy called, "Cut!"

"Leaf blower is really loud next door, dudes. We can't work like this."

Kim turned to me. "Felicia, you need to go charm your neighbor, get the gardener to stop working."

"But why me?!"

"It's your neighbor."

"Oh, God. Okay."

When I send food back at a restaurant . . . well, I don't. Because I'm convinced they'll send it back with cyanide in it. Or bodily fluids. I have only fired agents by certified letter. I apologize to cashiers when I return things at clothing stores. *I'm sorry you have to re-rack this dress because of me, but look! I steamed the wrinkles out!* Confrontation is what I dread the most in life. But my precious creation needed me to gird my loins. So that's what I did.

I walked next door with my heart pounding in my throat. This was how Marie Antoinette had approached the guillotine, I was sure of it. "Hi, Mr. Gregory! We're filming over at my house . . ."

"Is that why people were loud at seven a.m. this morning?" Of course, he had to embody the "cranky old man neighbor" cliché.

"Um, so sorry, I'll tell them to be quiet tomorrow. We just need to finish filming."

"So?"

"And we need the leaf blower to stop blowing?"

"He has to finish. The crepe myrtle's gone crazy this year. When I first planted that tree . . ."

"What a cool story. Ahem, so if he could just pause for thirty minutes or so . . ."

"Don't ask me, ask him."

I turned to the gardener, who was standing too close, staring at me silently, and holding the leaf blower on his shoulder like a weapon. I started sweating.

"Hello." No response. "Can you wait for thirty minutes please before doing more leaf blowing?"

He stared at me. And stared. I turned to Mr. Gregory.

"Does he speak . . ."

Mr. Gregory was staring at me, too. I felt like I was in a zombie movie. I fumbled in my pocket for any money I had and held out my hand.

"Eleven dollars? Stop blowing? Until five o'clock?" I tapped my wrist. There was no watch there.

The gardener took the money and nodded.

"Thank you, Mr. Gregory!" I called out over my shoulder as I ran away as fast as I could, back into my house. Full run. (Reminder, I have no dignity.)

Kim met me at the door. "How'd it go?"

"He'll stop for a half hour, but I'm pretty sure if my house is invaded by robbers in the future, he'll lend them a dolly to help carry stuff to their car. Let's make this COUNT!"

Every time the camera rolled on set, my nerves ratcheted up. I seriously didn't poop for a week. I think it was because I cared SO MUCH. I wanted everything to be perfect, I wanted people to think we were hilarious; hell, I wanted us to be the first to win an Oscar for a web series. I had incredibly high expectations, and at the same time, I wasn't secure in anything I was doing. Half the time I put my "producer hat" on, I felt like I was playing dress-up.

"Absolutely the budget can accommodate a Steadicam for this shot. Psst, Jane: What's a Steadicam?"

I pretended to be a leader, but on the inside I was still that home-schooled kid who wasn't allowed to walk to the corner by herself. Because, you know, murderers.

I knew I was a jittery mess, so I tried to self-coach myself off the ledge every morning, *Be happy! All the work we're doing is so good! Remember? That chauvinist comment from Bladezz yesterday went over like gangbusters!* But as a superstitious Southern lady, any second of enjoying myself felt like I was deliberately inviting disaster into the production. So any positivity backfired.

The whole time on set, I was convinced that something terrible was going to happen. So I coped by visualizing every horrific scenario possible and playing it out blow-by-blow in my mind as I tried to get to sleep at night. I saw the police shutting us down when a PA double-parked outside, a tsunami hitting Los Angeles before we got to film episode two. I had a recurring dream that one of the actors, Jeff Lewis, would have a heart attack. Or an aneurysm. He was the highest-risk cast member. Almost forty, practically a corpse. So every morning I'd look up "instant death" diseases on my phone in order to say them out loud to myself in the bathroom mirror and prevent disaster from killing him and ruining my show.

"Blood clot."

"Aneurysm."

"Heart attack."

"Stroke . . ."

Knock on the door. "Felicia, are you ready to roll?"

"Sure!" <whispers "morphine overdose" into mirror> "Okay! I'm ready!"

This sounds insane, I know, but I do this ritual a lot. When I'm driving in a thunderstorm, I say out loud to myself in a very musical theatre voice, "Gee, I sure hope this rain doesn't make me spin out of control and make me die on this highway!"

Laugh if you will; I've never had a spinout. Or had an actor die of a web-series aneurysm.

[5: Making Things with Friends Is Awesome]

Even though every single second of filming was stressful and panicked and done completely illegally and the very hardest way, I'd never felt more alive doing anything in my life. There was a joy that I'd never felt before, because I was PLAYING with my friends. Many times during shooting, my fellow cast members were so funny I had to chant, *Dead kittens, dead kittens, dead kittens* for twenty seconds in my brain to get through a scene without giggling. Those were the moments I'll never forget. (Partially because of the traumatic visuals, partially because of the fun.)

We filmed for four days in the summer of 2007 and completed everything we aimed to do with the first few episodes of the script. There were complications, of course, like when I discovered that most of the cast had never played a video game before, but I just put on the hat of "gamer consultant" (in addition to lead actress, show runner, and co-caterer) and plowed ahead.

"What does this term mean?"

"You won't understand. Just think, 'He has a Marc Jacobs purse and I want it.' "

"Got it!"

Looking back at those first episodes now, I see all the rough edges in the acting and the writing and the editing I never noticed at the time. But the fun we had making it blasts away the imperfections. Kim, Jane, the cast and crew, and I created something together that didn't exist before. Without permission. Without regrets. Hell, yeah.

8

WE MADE SOMETHING! #lookit

The fine art of grassroots "getting all up in people's faces" with *The Guild*. Tweetin' and pioneerin' and awards! Oh my!

When I was in music school in college, everyone had to perform a senior recital in order to complete their degree. But it was a serious pain to get anyone to ATTEND the events. Enduring a classical saxophone concert for more than fifteen minutes is a private hell NO ONE wants to live through if you're not dating the person, believe me.

As the tiny prodigy of the building, I entered my recital semester with an ego the size of a Mack Truck. There was no way I was playing to an empty house! Did I put eight months of work into learning a Henryk Wieniawski showpiece with twelve million notes packed into three minutes for nothing? Hell, no! *People were gonna show up. They had no mother-frakkin' choice!*

Ahem.

I did all the regular things you were supposed to do to get attendance. I ordered tons of food and picked out a skanky dress that my professor gave two thumbs-up to, but I knew I needed something extra. Something special. Maybe something to do with the fliers everyone posted around campus to advertise their events? I asked myself, *What can I make that stands out from the boring "John Smith plays an evening of Brahms at 7 p.m. Tuesday" kind of thing?*

Hmm, what could I do . . . ?

Tune in to...
felicia
warrior violinist

April 29 at 5:30
Recital Studio
Music Recital Hall

Yup, that'll work. That's me as "Xena, Princess Violinist." I whipped it up in the computer lab one evening, and, MAN, was I happy when I figured out how to engulf that violin in flames. An evil genius "muhahaha" kind of joy!

I printed up about a hundred of the fliers and blanketed the music building at 11:00 p.m., right before the place locked up. I couldn't wait to see what people thought when I got to school the next day.

Good news: THEY PAID ATTENTION.

Bad news: I got pulled into the dean's office and was forced to take the fliers down due to "questionable taste level." But at that point there weren't many left anyway. People had stolen them. All the stoner percussionist majors tracked me down to say, "Badass, man, I'll be there!"

For once in my weirdo too-young-for-collegiate-life . . . I felt cool.

And yes, I sold out the venue.

People ask me if I have a marketing or PR background, since that's what helped catapult *The Guild* into situational internet fame against all odds. Answer? Nope, I have no qualifications in those areas. But I've always had a flair for showmanship. I love adding a bit of "VOILÀ!" to life, like secretly slipping a turd into the pool and watching people react REALLY strongly. Um, except it's a turd everyone gets excited about, not grossed out by. One made of gold or diamonds or something . . . I dunno where this analogy is going.

Kim, Jane, and I had a meeting right after we finished filming to figure out what we were going to do with the show. We knew the episodes were going to be great, but any plans after that? Not so much.

I tried to be organized and take charge. I even brought a clipboard to the meeting. "So we have a show to release . . ."

Kim nodded. "And?"

"Uh, that's all I got. What do we do with it?" I dropped my clipboard next to me in the booth, because I suddenly felt stupid for bringing a clipboard into a coffee shop. Or owning a clipboard at all.

Jane said, "We need a plan to get people to see the show before we upload it next week. Kim, how did your video do so well?"

"It's quirky. And it was linked by a TV show," said Kim.

"And it has a character named Lick Poop."

I frowned. "I don't think we can count on the viral thing happening like that with this show."

"Don't sell yourself short. Episode two has great poop jokes."

"Meh. They're okay." I was always the gloomy Darth Vader of the group. I could even see the dark side of poop jokes.

"We could use help in the PR department. Does anyone know anyone?"

"For free? I already called in every favor for dog, cat, house-, or baby-sitting during filming. Every single sitting favor I had. Tapped out."

Jane sighed. "Well, someone has to be in charge of outreach. Or no one will ever see what we've made."

There was a long pause where we sipped our lattes together, knowing someone needed to step up to the plate, but no one wanting to fall on this particular sword.

At last, I raised my hand. Like I was in English class. What a dork. "Uh, I'll do it. Because I know the internet best? Kinda?"

With that overconfident hubris, I went home and tried to conquer the fantastic world of online marketing! My only starting point was, "People. Want to make them watch things. How do I corral them?" Since the internet is part egalitarian democracy, part vengeful cat worshipers, it was a daunting task. Because I knew that making something discoverable on the web is like sending someone on a scavenger hunt into the universe's biggest flea market. There's anything and everything available you can imagine, with an infinite number of stalls to browse and no emergency exits in sight. (That sentence flashed me back to a trip I took to Ikea recently. Major panic attack in the cutlery section.)

But it was actually the perfect time to dive in, because 2007 was when social startups were popping up online like acne on a teenager's face. It's hard to imagine with babies practically born with hashtags tattooed on their foreheads today, but social media back then was not mainstream. Twitter and Facebook and Tumblr, most of those sites were brand spanking new. They were super nerdy, super fringe, and super small. (The trending topics were like Drupal and the latest version of Linux. So yeah. That nerdy.) And I had a secret power in this new world: I was used to trolling the internet desperately for friends. (In 2002, I had a Friendster account, yo.) So all the experience I'd had hanging out online and creating bitchin' recital fliers was about to pay off!

I sat down and scoured the web for every single social network startup that was able to reach new people for free and jumped on them to claim the usernames /felicia and /theguild. Ever go into a gas station and browse the souvenir section for a key chain or a coffee cup with your name on it, only to discover your parents were horrible human beings and named you too weird to be part of the rest of civilization? That's what I experienced every time I had to settle for /feliciaday and /watchtheguild instead. (To the girl who has /felicia on Twitter: Damn you, ma'am. Damn you to hell.)

I also taught myself how to program a website. In the most rudimentary, janky, kid-with-crayons way. I've always taken my art seriously, even when I was terrible at it. From ages eight to twelve, I would spend months making everyone in my family handmade gifts for Christmas:

"Mom, get in the car, let's go! I need more blue construction paper."

"You have a ton of paper there."

"But I'm out of royal blue. Santa is flying through the night sky to deliver presents, it's 2:42 a.m. GMT in this piece, I need blue!"

"Can't you use black?"

"He's flying through *Norway*. Notice the fjords I created with hundreds of individually cut-out gray mosaic pieces? It's daylight there in the winter, it would be untruthful to have the night sky be so dark. GIVE ME THE TOOLS FOR GRANDMA'S PRESENT, MOM! DON'T NEUTER MY VISION!"

With that kind of intensity, I binged fifty hours of online video tutorials and used my "skills" to make something that turned out one step above GeoCities level.

I was so proud. I printed out a screenshot and taped it on the fridge. Then I sent this email to the ladies after I uploaded the design files. Quote:

We're ready to release! The website's up. AND I made us a Myspace!

XOXO

Felicia

Unquote.
Unironic.

And as my marketing coup d'état, the day we released the first episode of *The Guild* I sat in my computer chair for eighteen hours using all the accounts I'd created to bother people all across the internet. In the most inefficient way possible.

I wrote messages to hundreds of bloggers at gaming-related websites and linked them to the first episode of *The Guild*. But instead of using a form letter (cut and paste was too sophisticated for me at that point), I typed each email individually. Because I didn't want to come across as "fake." (Even though I essentially wrote the same thing to each person.)

I also went overboard on the hard sell. Just a little.

"Dear sir/ma'am, My name is Felicia Day, I have been an actress on such TV shows as *Buffy the Vampire Slayer* and have recently written a show based on the game World of Warcraft. Here is a link and another five paragraphs about how great it is. Plus, I tailored this email to your specific tastes because I researched every single one of your blog posts on the internet and have files of screenshots from your personal Facebook. Please spread word about my show because I know everything about you and have a general idea of where you live. That's not creepy, right?"

It sounds counterintuitive (and illegal), but my spamming worked. And not just in a "restraining order" way! More and more people started watching and linking the video. Bloggers who must have had a high "creep" tolerance posted about it, and that led to more views, and the cycle kept repeating itself. So I just sat there and kept emailing. And emailing. The process morphed into a game for me. With my WoW addiction dead and buried, I'd finally found a legitimate reason to sit at the computer for hours. I even bought a pair of those compression socks. You know, to prevent blood clots from sitting too long.

In the "getting views" department, I had no shame.

"Yes, Grandma, that's the right video, the one with my face. Now all you have to do is hit the triangle and play the video. And when it stops, just play it over and over again."

"How many times, hon?"

"All day every day. Have Poppy do it on his computer, too. Love you!"

I forced all my relatives and friends to go through YouTube view-scumming training. I probably contributed ten thousand views to the show myself, running the show on mute in the background of my browser as I replied day and night with a personal "Thank you!" to every single blog entry, forum comment, or tweet related to the show. I needed to convey personally to every single person in the world HOW AWESOME *THE GUILD* WAS. DO YOU HEAR ME, WORLD? IT'S AWESOME! *HAVE SOME MORE CAPS!*

I think part of why I glommed on to the task so much (besides more than a touch of OCD) is because crusades are part of my DNA. My mom was into politics my whole life, and I have vivid memories of helping her stuff envelopes as a preschooler in the "John Glenn for President" headquarters while Michael Jackson played on the radio. She always worked for a losing, underdog candidate, and was super active in the Independent Ross Perot campaign in 1992. (How do I describe this . . . it was the Tea Party movement of the early '90s? Tons of people just got angry at me. Oh, well.)

We would hold signs on street corners, travel over state lines to rally after rally (thanks to the "illegally not attending school" thing), all the while believing that we had the power to tear the establishment down. Advocating for my own web show kinda felt like standing on a street corner all day, handing out fliers, takin' down "the man." And the minute real actual humans started responding back, well, that's when I truly got hooked. Viva la Webolution!

"Mississippians for Perot"
Because being for Perot
wasn't quite hick enough.

It was thrilling to refresh the video page over and over again and see comments roll in about our work. I'd love to say Kim and Jane and I focused on the compliments, but it's the internet. You can't help but pay attention to the mean things more. We traded the "best" back and forth:

> "Webisode . . . uh . . . no. Which writer from *MADtv* wrote this?"
>
> ". . . which high-school did you get those actors out of?"
>
> "that's the lady from the T-Mobile commercial. And the *Transformers* Chevy commercial. What a low-rent bitch."
>
> "wasn't really funny, but the girl was decent." *Or to put it in words the OT can comprehend* "I'd pee in her butt."

But whatever was written, it was feedback. And I discovered that internet feedback, in any format, is pretty seductive.

I don't say this to exaggerate the feel-goods, but the day we uploaded the first episode of *The Guild* was the day my life was transformed. Outside the fun of making it, we also had the faint hope in the back of our minds that someone "mainstream" would see the show and say, "Hey! Let's take this *Guild* thing off the internet and put it on television!" But as soon as I saw the view count tick upwards and the comments section fill up with "Hey, I'd do that chick!," the people I wanted to please in life shifted from Hollywood insiders, who'd shoved me into the quirky secretary box for so many years, to the people online who actually liked what I was doing. Or hated it. Either way, the feeling of "THEY LIKE US, KINDA!" was magical.

A week after our third (and last) episode was uploaded, I was acting in a terrible, low-budget Western movie. The kind you see in the bargain bin and say, "Wow that looks cheap." While riding to set in a van, wearing a hideous prairie woman outfit, my phone started going crazy, buzzing like a lady's pleasure toy with text after text.

"You're on the front page of YouTube!"

"Your face is on YouTube!"

"Do you have a show on YouTube? I swear this is you on the front page!"

Back then, YouTube handpicked cool videos to share with the community on the front page. Most old-school YouTube stars were created this way. And on that day in late 2007, our hard work was blessed by their magic wand.

It paid off big-time.

Tons of people found us through that featured spot. Seeing "Where's the next one?!" typed in the comments section over and over wasn't a BAD thing for the ego. Our views for the first episode skyrocketed past one million, and the brand-new episode three was up 200,000 in twelve hours. With that boost, I knew someone would be knocking on our door to help us make more episodes!

I held up the phone to the other actors in the van. "My show is on the front page of YouTube!"

They all looked over at me, confused. "You can make a show for the internet?"

[A Series of "You Go, Girl!" Events]

After the influx of fairy godmother YouTube views, we were able to get a snazzy Hollywood agent and started taking meetings with "the fancies" to pay for more episodes. I won't lie; it was pretty awesome to be courted. I'd always wanted a "coming-out" party, like seventeen-year-olds had in Regency romance novels. Taking meetings around town felt like my version of being presented to the Queen. I always held my left hand out like it should be kissed when I was introduced to people at meetings. "Lovely to meet you, sir and/or madam." (No one ever kissed it. The hoi polloi are so uncouth.)

The truth was, we were like the pauper girl trying to snag a prince. We literally didn't have any money to make even ONE more episode on our own. But we thought by meeting with tons of web video companies and networks, someone would just write us a check, no strings attached, so we could get on with filming our next season. *Fund us! Our hymen is intact, take us to the altar, Prince Hollywood!*

The first episode of *The Guild* is titled "Wake-Up Call." That's exactly what I got out of those meetings.

"But I don't understand why you have to own the show completely." I squinted at the digital executive across from me. We were meeting for breakfast in a douchey hotel restaurant, and for the fiftieth time I thought to myself, *Why am I bothering with this Hollywood meeting thing again? Oh, right. I have to, if I want to keep making my show.*

"Writers don't own their work in this business." He patted me on my hand, and I looked down, wanting to wipe it on my jeans.

"But there wouldn't BE a show if it wasn't for the person who thought it up in the first place."

He smiled condescendingly. "The show wouldn't get made without the producer and network, though. We provide the money. It's 101."

Did he seriously just throw a "101" at me? How dare he. I have a 4.0! I leaned forward. "But it says here you can't guarantee me to star if it ever goes to TV. That's the whole point of why I wrote . . ."

"Don't worry, those issues are way down the line! We'll cross that bridge when we get to it." His "Aren't you cute!" attitude was really starting to piss me off.

"But . . ."

"We're offering to fund your show! Doesn't that make you happy?"

"You're giving me two thousand dollars a season. Total."

He leaned forward conspiratorially. "Since we're gonna work together, tell me the truth. You didn't ACTUALLY write this yourself, did you?"

"Huh?"

"I mean, girls don't really game, so . . ."

What. An. Asshole.

We got about a dozen offers for the show, opportunities most people trying to make it in Hollywood would kill for. Every time we got an offer, I tried to tell myself, *Yay, you did it! You're on the path to get in that hot tub with Johnny Depp! Accept the deal, fool!*

Then, when the paperwork finally hit my desk . . . I couldn't bring myself to sign.

I think at the heart of it, I was afraid that by giving up control, I would lose the sense of fulfillment I'd found through making *The Guild*. Working on the show meant more to me than a business deal. It felt like I'd finally found what I'd been searching for ever since I left my violin career behind: a sense of purpose. Of meaning. That the blind leap of faith I took after college, with all the ups and downs, had been worth it.

And I couldn't help feeling a little snotty. *What are these fancy-pants companies doing on the internet that's better than what we're doing on our own? None of them has produced web shows BIGGER than what the three of us have built in our garages. We can keep doing this ourselves, surviving on hoagies and favors . . . somehow!* Was I being delusional?

Yeah. I was.

During one of our last pitch meetings, a nice female executive who wasn't as slick as the rest said, "We can't invest right now, but why don't you ask your fans to help you out?"

Kim and Jane and I nodded and said, "What a great idea!" and then looked at each other as we left. "Is that chick nuts?"

This was the end of 2007, before Kickstarter or Indiegogo existed (they started in 2009 and 2008 respectively), so the idea that random people would be willing to help us fund videos was ridiculous. I mean, she might as well have suggested standing on the corner of an intersection with an "Unemployed, Need Help with Web Series!" sign. I was willing to do that, but didn't think I'd get a lot of donations on the corner of Vine and Sunset. For my vagina, yes. A web series? Nope.

But after a few more suit-douche meetings, I got desperate. And thought, *Sure! Let's go cyber-panhandling!*

I added a PayPal donation button to the sidebar of our website, right above our crucial Myspace icon. I had no expectations and did very little to publicize the button. The only perk I offered was that if you donated, you got your name listed in the show credits. I created all the credit pages in Photoshop myself, and sticking them on the ends of the videos was a pain. But I was willing to put in a small amount of effort. Even if I had to study more stupid video tutorials.

The next morning, I woke up to dozens of emails in my in-box. *Donation notifications? What the hell?!* Within two weeks we had enough money to make another episode. Even arrogant little me couldn't believe it. I called up Kim.

"Uh, we have enough money to shoot another episode."

"What? How? With the PayPal thingie?"

"Yup."

"That is so weird!"

"I KNOW!"

The process was surreal. And it made me paranoid. I was sure someone was playing a trick on us, like when I was ten, and my mom was certain that the Cuban mafia was conspiring to kidnap us into prostitution when we won a "Pick 3" lottery ticket in Florida. I could smell the same kind of nonconspiracy here, and I was not going to be taken in! When one dude in Indonesia donated three hundred dollars, I emailed him back immediately.

"Hello, thank you for your donation, I think your decimal point was in the wrong place? Happy to refund if it was a mistake! BTW, not traveling to Indonesia anytime soon, and no, you can't have my address or phone number."

It wasn't a mistake. People were willing to support us in order to make more *Guild*. Of their own volition.

It was the best compliment I ever got.

In total we had about five hundred people donate over six months, enough to fund the rest of my pilot script, rewritten and expanded into ten episodes. We didn't collect enough to pay the actors (or ourselves), but we were able to bring on more crew to help us, pay for locations outside our own houses, and buy a boom microphone that wasn't held together with duct tape. Toward the end of the first season, I even had to take the PayPal button off the website.

Why? Because so many people kept donating, I couldn't fit all of them into the end credits. That was smarter than, you know, LENGTHENING THE CREDIT MUSIC TO FIT MORE DONORS, FELICIA.

Viewer by viewer, our show was proving that we didn't need the Hollywood establishment in order to succeed. We were gonna break the system and take over the world!

Thank you, Ross Perot!

[Bad Ideas Seem Good Sometimes!]

"I can't go on, Kim. I just can't."

We were sitting in the middle of my kitchen floor, the linoleum tiles covered with DVDs stacked five feet high around us. Kim was operating the label maker (that took us two days to figure out how to set up), and I was filling out my fiftieth customs form of the day. By hand. I'd never sent anything overseas before, or I'd have told our international customers to go to hell. No offense.

Kim reached over and patted my shoulder.

"We're almost finished. Two more piles for today!"

"But it's so much. My hand is cramping. I . . . I can't do it anymore. Whose idea was this DVD thing in the first place? Oh, God, it was mine. Why do people in Israel want to watch our show? I can't fill out another form, I just can't!" Tears exploded from my face.

If you live in Israel and received a *Guild* season 1 DVD and your ink was smudged, now you know why. I'd reached my manual labor tipping point.

Over the summer of 2008, we continued taking meetings about the show, but at that point we'd stopped counting on a big company to come in and help us keep filming. We knew we could keep *The Guild* going. All by our lady lonesomes.

Of course, we needed to somehow get money to back-pay the cast so they'd keep working with us. (A year seemed kind of excessive to go without being compensated.) I hadn't had an acting job in a while because I was so busy online cheerleading for the show 24/7. So all that was a problem . . . yeah . . .

"We could make a DVD and sell it to fund another season? Would that work?" During a breakfast burrito brainstorming session with Kim, I threw that out, not knowing how it could be achieved, but it sounded smart to my ears.

Kim thought about it for a second. "People like DVDs. Yeah! Let's do it."

At that point we were high on our own independence. Empowered anarchists. We could do anything!

Oh, boy.

I wrote season two of the show while Kim tried to figure out how to make a DVD from scratch. (Jane had moved on after season one to direct other things.) Heads up: There are jobs that you can DIY, and there are others that are worth paying someone else to do. DVD fulfillment is one of those you should NEVER TRY BY YOURSELF

UNLESS YOU THINK PUNCHING YOURSELF IN THE FACE IS A FUN WEEKEND ACTIVITY.

I changed the PayPal button on the website to be a preorder for the DVD and estimated we'd sell around a hundred copies. There were more than a thousand orders in a week. It was a sphincter-puckering windfall. The plan had always been to send them out ourselves, but never at that volume. After endless stuffing and addressing of envelopes and the inevitable "Oops, Kim! I forgot to charge people shipping!," I'd reached my limit.

Kim sat down next to me and tried to calm me down, as usual.

"Would you rather be at a fast-food commercial audition?"

"No."

"Would you rather have sold the show and have other people tell us what to do?"

"No." Sniff.

"Then we'll finish these DVDs, back pay the cast, then invest our share back into the show, and start shooting again. Does that sound like a plan?"

"Yes. Good plan. Yes."

"Maybe we can ask some volunteers from Twitter to come help us with the labeling."

"Better plan, yes."

"Give me the customs forms, I'll do the rest."

Kim grabbed my pile of papers and shoved the return address stamper at me instead. "Stamp for a while. It's therapeutic. Pretend you're mushing it on somebody's face."

I stamped a few dozen packages imagining I was mushing the face of that particularly annoying douche-suit guy I'd met, and it helped. She was right. Damnit.

As the DVD orders slowed to a trickle, I finished writing the script for *The Guild* season two and we prepped to shoot the first episode on our DVD savings. It was going to be the shoestring way again, with only a few hoagies to split amongst everyone for lunch, but that was the only way to do it. We'd go for as long as we could! Or something plan-ish like that.

The week before we started shooting, I got a call from our snazzy Hollywood agent, George.

"Felicia, do you know Xbox?"

"Uh, of course I do. I'm a gamer. Duh."

"They want to talk about making new *Guild* episodes."

Ugh. I was so burned on meetings at that point, I got uppity.

"You know how I feel about . . ."

He was used to my antiestablishment tirades and interrupted before I could build up to my "strident" voice.

"They're willing to be flexible. Just take the meeting, please."

"Really?" A gaming company that would pay for the show and be okay with my anarchist demands? I decided to take the meeting. Because if nothing else, I thought, *Maybe I can scam a free Xbox!*

And over pancakes (because I ALWAYS take meetings over pancakes), surprise, surprise, the Xbox guy seemed . . . flexible. And not condescending. They didn't need to own the show, they'd leave creative decisions up to us, and they would give us a decent budget so we could pay everyone reasonably and feed them something besides cheap hoagies. In fact, they replied to literally everything I asked for with, "Sure, that's reasonable."

It made me flustered. Because it's one thing to ask for what you want and another thing to GET it.

Checkmate, Felicia Day.

And that's how we made four more seasons over four years with Xbox. Because I dug in my heels and was unreasonable, and got rewarded for it. (Definitely adding that to the coffee mug slogan bin.)

We started shooting the first two episodes of season two the weekend after the meeting, knowing that we would be 100 percent guaranteed to shoot the rest of the season, and no one on set would be working for free anymore. In a quiet moment during filming, I pulled Kim aside with tears in my eyes and hugged her.

"No more hoagies!" I whispered into her ear.

She nodded. "No more hoagies."

Over the next several years, we found more ways to pioneer in the world of web video. I wrote a *Guild* comic book series, the show was the first web series released on Netflix. We even released a music video single that was number one on iTunes for a week. Beat Taylor Swift. (A song that was recorded in a friend's closet, staring at his socks.) Sure, all the business things we did with *The Guild* are cool, but it was the relationship that developed between us and the fans and, for me, my own family, that made every rebellious step of the way worth it.

One of the drawbacks of being a homeschooled kid was that I don't think I learned to be as independent as regular kids. My mother got me into violin, my grandfather got me into math, I killed myself getting a 4.0 in college; a lot of my life I did things because OTHER people guided my behavior. When I dove into acting with such naïve confidence, for the first time I was following something for myself. Problem was, my family didn't understand the movie business, so they worried. A lot. Chances were high in their minds that I might end up becoming a porn actress and/or a heroin addict. (They had seen that happen once on *Law & Order*.)

When I tried to prove to them, "Hey! This is the thing I'm meant to do!" I'd frequently get egg on my face, like when I made everyone stay up until 12:01 a.m. to watch my first professional job, a Starburst commercial, not knowing I'd gotten cut completely out of it. My mom was confused.

"Where were you? Did I miss you?"

"No. I guess I got cut out of it, Mom."

"Oh, honey. What happened? Were you bad?" Mortifying.

Over the years, when my career didn't seem to be building to anything significant, my dad in particular became a fan of the "backup plan." He's a very practical and business-savvy guy, and in a helpful way he hinted here and there in phone calls, "If you need to come home, I'll pay for your law school . . ."

In the lowest days of my career, I thought about taking him up on it.

But then *The Guild* took off, and it finally seemed to prove that I'd chosen the right path. The problem was that the internet world was so new, it was hard to make my family understand, "We're on YouTube and Xbox now! It's a gaming console. Yes, it's for games but they also have video . . ." meant I was guaranteed to not move into their spare bedroom anytime soon.

I was in Austin, Texas, visiting my dad around season three of *The Guild*, and we ended up going to Bed Bath & Beyond together, probably for a new griddle because he's a real "cook the sausage until they turn into meteorites" kind of guy. I could tell he wanted to talk to me about something serious. He's always trying to get me to save money for some reason, so I thought, *Ugh, another time where I have to pretend to understand what he's talking about with 401(k)s.*

As we wandered the aisles, of course I shoved things into the cart I wanted for myself so he'd pay for them. (I don't care how old you are, that's a daughter privilege.) He cleared his throat, and I knew he was going to launch into it.

"Honey, I want you to know you can always come home. Uh, you know. If things aren't working out."

I stopped the cart and rolled my eyes. I definitely would have rather talked with him about a 401(k) thingie. "Things are working out, Dad. I'm fine!"

"You haven't been on TV as much lately."

"Well, I've been working on all my internet stuff."

"That sounds fun, but are you making a living at it?"

"I . . . kinda." Technically I was still paying most of my bills with commercial acting, but unless I was phoning home for a check, he didn't need to know that.

"I'm just saying, UT Law School is one of the best in the country. You always liked that *Ally McBeal* show . . ."

"Dad! I'm doing great! Honest . . ."

"Hey! Are you . . . Codex?"

We had stopped to have our earnest Lifetime moment in the linens section, and a guy in his early twenties wearing a polo shirt peered out at us from behind a stack of flamingo beach towels.

I smiled. "Uh, yeah! That's me."

"Wow, this is so cool!"

He walked over, and my dad looked at the guy skeptically. I had a feeling he thought the guy was a plant.

"I love your show! I'm working, so it's not technically allowed, but think I could get a picture with you?"

"Sure!"

As we posed in front of a stack of "As Seen on TV" items, my dad took the photo, then handed the phone back to the kid.

Dad had a weird look on his face. "You've really seen her web show?"

"Yeah! Me and my roommate love it. We're gamers. Bought the DVDs!"

"That's awesome, thanks for supporting!" I smiled and high-fived him. For many reasons, I'd never loved a stranger more than in that moment.

The guy waved and started to leave. "Nice to meet you! The roommate is never gonna believe this!"

As he walked away, my dad looked at me, and there was something different in his eyes. Surprise. Shock. And more than a little bit of admiration.

"That was pretty cool."

"Yeah."

"Ahem."

There was an awkward beat between us. Was he gonna bring up the law school thing again? Ask me more about my show? Talk to me about my pension benefits?

"Let's go get some pancakes." He put his arm around me, and we pushed the cart toward the checkout. A few aisles later I had to pretend to look at ShamWows to wipe away a few tears.

Yeah, that moment near the flamingo beach towels was my sweetest *Guild* victory of all.

- 9 -

Convention Fevah

I have a cabinet filled with dolls of myself
in my office. But I didn't MAKE any of them,
so that makes it less creepy, right?

In the summer of 2008, I walked onstage with the cast and creators of *Dr. Horrible's Sing-Along Blog*, a musical web series released on the internet just weeks before, and was greeted by the screams of more than five thousand people. We were at San Diego Comic-Con, in Ballroom 20, the second largest hall at the biggest nerd event in the world. With me were Nathan Fillion and Simon Helberg and Neil Patrick Harris, my *Horrible* costars, and Joss Whedon and his siblings, Zack, Jed, and Jed's wife, Maurissa, the writers. Joss Whedon was also the director. You may be familiar with him from *Buffy the Vampire Slayer*, *Firefly*, and *The Avengers*. (Whew, that was a lot of name-dropping.) As I smiled and waved to the audience, gazing out on the huge room filled with thousands of faces, I suddenly knew what it felt to be a rock star.

And my inner dik-dik didn't want any terrifying part of it.

Nathan and Neil and Joss were extremely witty onstage during the panel, bantering with one another like the superstars they are, and the only thing I could do was stare down at the iPhone 3G in my lap, frozen in fear. After the initial semi-thrill of walking onstage, five thousand people staring at you comes with an intimidating amount of eyeball reflection. At a certain point, a question got thrown to me, but there was an awkward beat of silence on stage because I wasn't paying attention. I was busy staring at my lap. Nathan leaned forward to cover for me as I looked up and blurted out, "Oh! I'm sorry, what was the question? I was . . . Twittering under here."

This was 2008. Not a lot of nontech people were on Twitter at that point. So it sounded . . . suggestive.

Yup, people thought exactly what you'd think "twittering" was if you didn't know about social media: they thought I was masturbating under the table. And so did Nathan.

"It's hot in here," I said, flustered by the roar of laughter from the crowd.

"And wet," said Neil. Which made me turn as pink as my borrowed designer sweater.

After that, a lot of fans joined Twitter.

Once I recovered from hyperventilating in shame, we finished the panel and went to sign posters. Hundreds of fans shuffled through our line, jostling one another and the table, with security guards struggling to hold the crowd in check. When my hand started to cramp from signing and I developed a crazy tic over my right eye from smiling too hard, I wondered, *How did THIS become part of my life?*

[Fan by Fan]

I attended my first fan convention during college. It was the South Texas Amphibian and Lizard Show, held in the run-down ballroom of an Austin Hilton. No, I wasn't a toad collector at any point (although that wouldn't surprise you, would it?). I was there on a first date. I'd planned the whole thing myself and thought it was a creative way for two people to get to know each other. Afterward, we went to a staging of *Antigone* performed in ancient Greek, and for dinner I found an Ethiopian restaurant where, per cultural tradition, we ate a feast only with our fingers.

Dude didn't ask me out again.

But I remember walking into the lizard convention, enchanted by how many people in Austin *loved* lizards. And amphibians. And spiders. And a lot of other things I didn't have any temptation to bring home with me. (When I was twelve, I had a pet boa constrictor, Stella, whom I loved until I realized it needed to eat LIVE ANIMALS to survive. My mom had to feed Stella just-born "pinkie" mice while I sobbed outside in the hallway. Thank God, she died of a mouth infection before she got big enough to eat animals with actual hair. SORRY, STELLA, IT WAS ME NOT YOU!)

My favorite part of the lizard event was standing near a group of guys at a meet-up in the hotel coffee shop, all with ginormous iguanas perched on their shoulders. They were discussing the best type of feed, what to do when your "friend" was molting, and breeding techniques. (I grabbed my Frappuccino and walked away at that point. Quickly.)

Even though it was hella strange, I loved the vibe of the event. There were so many people meeting to celebrate something they loved. I wanted to be a part of that. Without the iguana sex tips. I had no idea that years later, fan conventions of the GEEK kind would build my career more than anything else.

Despite most of the media attention centering around big Hollywood-driven events like San Diego Comic-Con, there are hundreds of smaller fan conventions taking place around the world every weekend, celebrating sci-fi, anime, Abraham Lincoln impersonators (yup): you name it, there's a fan convention for it. I've attended hundreds of these events as a guest, starting as an actor on the cult favorite *Buffy the Vampire Slayer*. When I started my web show *The Guild*, I continued attending. Even though people didn't know that it existed.

I called up Kim right after we launched.

"Hey! There's a World of Warcraft convention happening next week in Anaheim. I'm gonna make *The Guild* bookmarks and hand them out down there so gamers will watch the show."

"Bookmarks? What about postcards?" said Kim.

"They're twenty-three percent more expensive."

"Bookmarks sound great!"

I ordered two thousand of them and drove down to Anaheim. I didn't have a ticket to the convention—they'd sold out months in advance—so I stood in front and handed out my DIY bookmarks to everyone who went inside. The experience had to be like a college student working the sidewalk for Amnesty International: smiles greeted with hostility all the way!

"Hi! Would you like a bookmark? No? Okay."

"Hey, I'd love to talk to you about my . . . no, it's not a church thing . . ."

". . . it's a web series about gamers who play a game like WoW? No, I'm not a booth girl. Yes, I play the game. No, you can't test me . . ."

Ninety percent of my handouts got thrown in the trash. Most people did it right in front of me. But 10 percent seemed mildly interested in the show, and in the face of so much rejection, mild interest felt like a huge win! After dark, I collected all the discarded bookmarks that didn't have gum stuck on them and drove home, vowing to canvass more events in the future. (I got rid of the extras by placing stacks of them on the doors of public toilets. Captive audience, yo!)

During the first few seasons of the show, I lived the life of an old-timey traveling salesman. I'd tweet, "Be in Seattle this weekend! Come on down! Buy more, get more discount! SALE SALE SALE!" and fans would let me crash their convention booths, dragging boxes of my *Guild* DVDs and comics as my "wares" (along with my face for selfies).

We even got ambitious for a few years and tried to run our own *Guild* booth at Comic-Con, sharing with my friend Jamie, a game designer. The experience did not go well. Our friendly indie fans generally got crowded out by mainstream fans lining up to get free life-size Harry Potter bags at the bigger movie studio booths.

"Hey, are you Emily Blunt?!"

"Definitely not. I'm here with my web show. Can I sell you a DVD?"

"Not unless you're Emily Blunt."

The last straw was when we decided one year to sell T-shirts and bought tons of Ikea shelving. Which I tried to assemble. By myself.

"Why are there so many pieces?! And there are no words to explain the pictures? Is it a secret IQ test?"

"No one knows," Jamie said.

I put a whole shelving unit together backward, and when I discovered I had to undo two hours of work, I started hyperventilating.

"Kim! I'm having flashbacks to DVD stuffing. No T-shirts! Never again!"

Eventually, our show got more popular, and the cast and I started to get invited to conventions legitimately as guests, all expenses paid, no Ikea shelving required. I guess coordinators saw the lines of fans waiting to meet me and thought, *That web series chick doesn't have a sales tax permit. Better give her an official spot before she gets arrested by the feds.*

By the 2010 San Diego Comic-Con, the most influential fan convention in the world, *The Guild* had grown in popularity enough to fill a three-thousand-seat panel room. More than some network TV shows. Not bad for a show that was shot in our garages, huh? (Yes, I've mentioned the garage thing too many times, but listen: we did all that stuff out of our garages.) At the same time I was doing my own show,

I was also acting on other sci-fi friendly shows. *Eureka. Supernatural.* And those projects, along with *Dr. Horrible* and my other web projects, bumped me pretty high up the "situational recognition" ladder at fan conventions not only in the US, but around the world.

It's a very strange experience to go back and forth between real life, where almost no one recognizes me except baristas, to events where 99 percent of people see me and think, *I know that chick! She's pale like the underbelly of a fish in person!* It's a shock to the ego.

They think I'm awesome!

Actually, I'm crap.

Correction! Awesome again!

Shut up, nobody.

As a self-conscious, I'm-sure-I-have-a-booger-in-my-nose kind of person, it was hard to get used to the scrutiny. When I first started doing speeches and panels, I'd constantly get flashbacks to the only high school event I ever attended.

It was a Valentine's dance and I was sixteen. An assistant instructor at my karate school, Juan, asked me to be his date. I was nervous because I'd never been INSIDE a public school before, but I said to myself, *He's a karate instructor, so if the jocks attack us, I should be safe.*

I asked, "What should I wear?" and he said, "It's Valentine's. The fanciest dress you have." No need to say it twice! I got the most beautiful green crushed-velvet dress, floor length, no back, jewels galore, mile-high heels; I even bought my own corsage. (I didn't know at the time those were supposed to be gifted to you by the guy. Oh well. I'm liberated.)

We entered the San Antonio High School gym dressed like we were meeting the Queen of England, and as I descended the steps, I gazed around the room. Everyone turned to stare at us. More than a hundred people. Not one dress in sight. Everyone was dressed in plain jeans and T-shirts. One person was wearing pajamas.

The kids pointed and whispered at us as we worked our way through the crowd. A few snickered. I had never been around this many kids my own age before. At that moment I understood exactly how Carrie must have felt at her prom.

I've gotten used to public speaking in front of thousands and spending an extra hour in the mirror every morning trying to decide if I'm overdressed or not now, but sometimes when I enter a convention floor and walk through the crowds, I have a traumatic flash of *Green velvet, green velvet!* zip through my brain.

It gets weirder when I meet celebrities whom I admire. Then my sense of identity really starts to cartwheel. I can't tell you how many times I've sat backstage feeling like an interloper who somehow made the convention invite list by accident. When someone I adore, like Gillian Anderson or William Shatner, enters the greenroom, I generally try to keep quiet and stand near the hummus, waiting for someone to say, "Oops. Someone invited the wrong 'Felicia.' Kick out that girl who's hogging all the pita chips."

I met Patrick Stewart one time, and when he started directing words toward my head, I became so light-headed I almost fainted. I kept repeating, "Would you like my chair? Would you like my chair?" until a volunteer came to extract him. Another time I got up two hours early, walked to a special donut shop four miles away from my hotel, and brought dozens of donuts to the convention for the EXPRESS purpose of carrying a box over to Matt Smith (Doctor Who #11) and asking, "Do you want one?" *Because I couldn't figure out how to introduce myself like a real human being.* (He did NOT want a donut. And he ended up thinking I was a volunteer, not a guest. For obvious reasons.)

The most mortifying incident was when I met Nichelle Nichols at a convention in Salt Lake City. She was wearing the most dazzling gold jacket I'd ever seen, sitting in a golf cart, glam as all get-out. I mean, *Lieutenant Uhura, in the flesh!* As I skirted around her golf cart in the hallway, I wanted to stare, willed myself not to, then compromised with a creepy side-eye look as I passed and then . . . she called out to me.

"Hi! Felicia! I wanted to meet you!" She waved.

I froze. She knew my name? No way. *No WAY.*

"Uh, you wanted to meet ME?! But . . . but . . . but . . ." *Mind melting . . . say something human being-ish.* "Hi?"

"Hello!"

Form words, Felicia . . . "Uh, your jacket is so pretty!"

"Thank you, dear."

"Your jacket is sparkly. So pretty." *Doh! I said that already. But it came out of my mouth again for some reason.* Flashbacks to Patrick Stewart situation. I wanted to die.

"Yes. You already said that."

Crap, she noticed. "I love your work."

"Thank you!"

My body started moving of its own volition, shifting weight back and forth, a move taken from a Motown group, while my mind seized up. *Say something smart, something more about how you love her work, except less general . . .* "Uh . . . you're in a golf cart!" NOT THAT! SHE MIGHT HAVE A HIP PROBLEM! WHY BRING THAT UP?!

"Yes, it's easier to get around the crowds this way."

I babbled. "I still can't believe you know my . . . why did you want to . . . I'm a big fan of your work!" *COMPLETE A SENTENCE, GOD!*

"Thank you!"

Mention your favorite episode of hers! No, for some reason, your mind isn't working. I am your mind, and I'm not working. I'm warning you, if you say something right now, you might accidentally say "Star Wars" instead of "Star Trek" and then you'll have to commit hari-kari, right here, right now in this hallway, so just compliment her jacket again . . . NO! WRONG CHOICE! NO-WIN CONDITION! AAAAAAAAAAAH!

"I have to pee. Nicetomeetyoubye!"

And I ran away. Like, full-tilt running down the hallway. If you haven't guessed already, it's a habit of mine. I never found out why she wanted to meet me, either. I felt so ridiculous that I sat on the toilet for fifteen minutes until I was able to rewrite the scene in my head into a more functional account of what happened so I could live with myself. (It included a conversation about her sister, who was once an actor in *The Guild*. Why couldn't I have remembered that during the panic attack? I'm the WORST!)

I'm sure the conversation wasn't that weird from her point of view (maybe) but from mine it was mortifying. All I wanted to have said was <u>one thing</u>, one simple thing to have her remember me. To make an impact. To summarize why I was having a loose-bowel situation just LOOKING at her in person. Because I admired her so much.

Those experiences make me appreciate every interaction I have with fans of my own work at conventions. I try to go out of my way to connect with each person as much as I possibly can despite the long lines and stifling crowds and people in cosplay with fake weapons who accidentally poke people in the eyes with rubber broadswords. Because that single moment you get with someone you admire is so important, I never want anyone to walk away feeling mortified like I generally do when meeting someone I fan over.

That's why, when I take pictures with people, I'm open to almost any request.

"Can I pick you up?"

"Yes!"

"Can I pretend to propose to you?"

"As long as it's not legally binding, ha!"

"Can you pretend to stab me with this light saber?"

"Which organ?"

"Can I put you in a headlock?"

Long pause. "Uh . . . sure! Why not."

Of course, it's hard to please everyone. Especially if you're entering/exiting a toilet stall and someone comes running up saying, "Oh my God, can I have a selfie with you here? So hilarious!" Or you see someone tweet, "Felicia Day was eating a salad while she signed autographs today. No respect for her fans." I WAS HUNGRY AND DIDN'T WANT PEOPLE TO WAIT IN LINE! (But I haven't eaten in public at a convention since, so good job, Tweeter! You showed me.)

If you've never been to one of these events, you probably have a very *Big Bang Theory* idea about the attendants and want to know, "What's the creepiest thing a fan's ever done to you?" Aside from a few restraining orders I can't legally talk about, I can relate a few standout oddball encounters.

One time a dude wanted to buy a lock of my hair for $1,000. And he wouldn't take no for an answer.

"You have a lot of hair, and my friend would be so happy! He loves you."

"I appreciate his appreciation, but I'm not selling you my hair."

"Just an inch. It's a lot of money!"

I tried to get the guy to move along in a way that he wouldn't feel ashamed about being creepy. (Which he totally was.) "I don't know him and wouldn't want anyone to be able to clone me, haha."

When I mentioned "cloning," the guy got WAY too excited. "Cloning would be AWESOME. I'd only need a fingernail, how's that for a compromise? Say five hundred dollars?"

At that point, I stopped worrying about his self-esteem. "Security!"

Another time I had a guy in his early twenties approach me and ask me to autograph his arm. I've signed a ton of babies, breasts, and Nintendo power gloves, so I was cool with it. Until he let slip, "I'm gonna go tattoo over it."

I withdrew the pen. "Um, I don't think you should do that, why would you do that? Do you really want to do that?"

"I'm a big fan. And my buddy bet me five hundred dollars that I wouldn't do it. I need you to sign because I could use the five hundred dollars for community college tuition."

I was conflicted. This guy wanted to disfigure his body permanently and was asking me to enable him.

On the other hand, I REALLY wanted to see what it would look like.

"Please?"

"For the record, I discouraged you!" I took his Sharpie and drew artistically on his right shoulder. All those hours I put into signing my signature over and over as a kid paid off. Nice swoops. Not too girly. Dare I say . . . tattoo worthy.

He left, supposedly for the tattoo shop, and I thought, *Cool! I just got pranked in a very flattering way!*

An hour later, the guy comes running back to my booth, sleeve rolled up over his shoulder. "I did it!"

Right there on his arm, raised and red, was a tattoo of my signature. Permanently inscribed. On a stranger's body. It felt like I'd secondhand branded him. Also, it occurred to me too late that I should be worried about checks being forged with his body part. Oh, well.

"Congrats! Go get that money from your friend! Here's a free DVD!"

And that should have been the end of it. Most people outside motorcycle relationships can't tell a story like that. But the best part happened the following week, when I got a tweet that was sad and sweet and horrible at the same time.

Hey, tattoo doing well, here's a pic to prove it's me. Sad thing, buddy refused to pay up. :(

Attached was a still red-angry picture of my signature. That was permanent. And in no way contributed to the guy's college education.

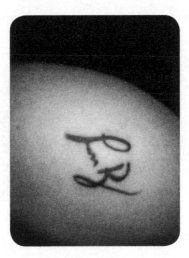

I laughed. Yes, I'm a terrible person.

Aside from outlier incidents like that (yes, I have more tattoo stories), all of my fans are interesting and enjoyable to meet. I've had fascinating conversations with writers, archaeologists, NASA/JPL engineers—all people I would never have known how to approach in real life, but I get to connect with now because of my work.

I think fan conventions are the epitome of what is fantastic about the internet. And probably why they've become so much more popular in the last several years. You're never weird when you're surrounded by people who are weird like you, right?

Conventions are a real-life slice of our digital lives. I feel at home when I walk onto a show floor and see all the booths carrying every *Doctor Who/Star Wars* mashup T-shirt invented. Where else can I buy a special set of dice that color coordinates with my character's hair or play a new video game next to a stranger who can appreciate the new armor designs as much as I do? That feeling I constantly get in everyday life of, *Oh boy, how do I connect with this stranger? Why don't they have a résumé attached to their forehead to help me out here with this dialogue thing?* is temporarily banished.

And, professionally, it means so much to meet people face-to-face and be reminded that the things I create can affect people's lives in small ways, too.

I have a picture framed on my office wall. A beautiful pastel print, blue and moody, of a female nude walking into a forest. It was given to me at a signing for my *Guild* comic book by a hip girl and a guy in their early twenties.

"We brought you something, Felicia. We're big fans." They lifted up a framed picture as they approached my table.

"This is beautiful! Thank you!" I took it from them, but I was puzzled. It wasn't the normal kind of fan art I usually received. (Not to be self-centered, but most of the stuff I'm given has my face on it.)

The girl indicated for me to turn the picture over. "Do you remember?"

Mounted on the back of the frame was a picture of a tweet I'd sent out two years before.

It referenced a blog article about a young woman, twenty-two, diagnosed with breast cancer, and her boyfriend, who was a game artist. He coordinated a huge gaming art auction to help pay off her medical bills. The cause spoke to me, and I tweeted it out. And that was it. I soon forgot about it. Two years later, the young woman hadn't.

"I'm her, I'm beautifulgrim. And your tweet helped the auction raise enough money to pay most of my medical bills." She pulled the guy she was with closer to her.

"This is my husband, he made the painting. We wanted you to have it, as thanks."

"Oh my God, that's you? Are you okay now?" She looked so

young. I couldn't believe she'd been diagnosed with breast cancer. It was awful. I was frozen just thinking of what she'd been through.

"I had a mastectomy and have been cancer-free for a year. Did you read what I wrote on the back?"

I looked down at the painting and read, "Your tweet helped me restore my hope when I was feeling lost."

And then I lost it.

I ran around the table and hugged her. I didn't know what else to do.

"I'm so glad you're better. Thank you." Encounters like that are unforgettable.

I've attended over a hundred conventions since 2007 and have had so many people share amazing stories with me. Big and small. Like a woman who was inspired to self-publish a novel because of my work, or a family who decided to paint video game characters on their kid's bedroom wall, despite never having picked up a paintbrush before. Or the dozens and dozens of web series that people have made because of what Kim and I did with *The Guild*.

At an event last year, I met a man in his late thirties, a big guy, who carried a poster roll and seemed nervous to approach. I shook hands with him over the signing table, trying to make him feel comfortable.

"Hi! My name's Felicia! How are you?!"

"Uh, okay. I'm just here to give you something." While talking, he started fumbling to open the poster tube. He was shaking. It wasn't smooth.

"Oh wow, I love presents! Not that I'm greedy, I'm polite when I take things from people. If they're free. Or not. I'll stop talking." Felicia Day, folks! Awkward, especially during public appearances!

He pulled out a poster from his tube and unrolled a print of me as

Codex, but done in a cool computer-art way, with a graphic style that was somewhere between pointillism and impressionism.

"This is gorgeous!" And it was. "Did you make this? Are you an artist?"

"Aw, no. I just drive a forklift at Costco. I'm not creative. I don't know how to do anything . . ."

"Wait, you aren't creative? But you made this." I held up the print.

"It was just in the computer."

"But it didn't exist before you turned the computer on and made it, right?"

"I guess."

"Then you created it." I was starting to get upset but kept myself in check. "Don't talk to yourself like that. You HAVE created things. You see the world in a unique way, and you expressed it right here in this poster."

"Well, I dunno. It's not good or anything."

"Well, I think it's good. But if you think that, you can get better. By doing more things, right?"

The guy nodded, uncomfortable. But I kept going. For some reason, it was important for him to understand what I was saying. (And I enjoy lecturing people.)

"Never put yourself down about things that you create. That mean voice inside you that says, 'You're not good enough' is not your friend, okay? I used to hear that voice all the time. If I hadn't started ignoring it, I wouldn't be here right now. Okay?"

"Okay." He started to shuffle backward. Probably scared. "Thanks for what you do, it's inspiring."

"Thank you for the poster!" I waved, then stood up. "Excuse me."

I walked behind the curtain of my booth and started bawling.

I wept for this guy, who was so vulnerable in front of me, and who, for some reason, felt the need to put himself down when he presented something he'd made from scratch. I don't let people get away with putting themselves down anymore. There are enough negative forces in this world—don't let the pessimistic voice that lives inside you get away with that stuff, too. That voice is NOT a good roommate.

A lot of people mock fandom and fan fiction, like it's lazy to base your own creativity and passion on someone else's work. But some of us need a stepping-stone to start. What's wrong with finding joy in making something, regardless of the inspiration? If you feel the impulse, go ahead and write that *Battlestar Galactica/Archie* mashup fiction! Someone online will enjoy it. (Especially if Archie gets ripped apart by Cylons.)

Over the years, I've received some of the most badass fan art you've ever seen. I have tons of dolls and paintings and sculptures of my characters in various projects that people have given me, made out of felt and plaster and pipe cleaners and poster board. I keep every single piece and put it in a storage unit that I pay WAY too much for every month for that sole purpose. This is partly because when fans give me things, it obviously means a lot to them and I don't want to have that go unrecognized. And partly because I once found a biography of Janice Dickinson in a Goodwill inscribed to an unnamed famous supermodel that said, "Love you forever!" I can't imagine how morti-fied Janice would be at finding her book given away, so I live in fear of that happening with a fan of mine. Personal guilt issues, I guess. (Side note: I also have props and clothing from all my projects I've acted in, just in case I'm homeless one day and need to eBay for food.)

In my home office, I have a cabinet dedicated to some of my favorite things people have given me over the years. It's not weird to have forty dolls of yourself staring at you, right? Please reassure me about this.

I like being able to see the pieces of art while I work. It reminds me of what's important about what I do.

Whether it was by someone volunteering to be an extra in our show, or part of the crew, or someone buying a DVD at a convention, or a superfan who tattooed our characters' faces on her calf, my career has been built fan by fan. I wouldn't trade that relationship, or collection of dolls of myself, for all the money and fame in the world.

The Deletion of Myself

That time I had a nervous breakdown and dreamt nightly of slashing my face with a straight razor while screaming, "DO YOU BELIEVE I NEED A BREAK **NOW,** GUYS?!"

I was born anxious. My mom must have watched a horror movie marathon while I was in utero or something, because I freak out at loud sounds, driving at night scares me because all the lights make me feel like I'm inside a UFO, and I'm traumatized, never delighted, by things that are startling. (SCREW surprise birthday parties.) My biggest fears in life are to be locked in a department store after hours, or to be kidnapped while walking to my car at night and my body disposed of with a wood chipper. Clearly, you can understand how challenging REAL problems are for me, like being late to a lunch meeting. "I'm sorry, I couldn't find a parking spot. Where would you like me to shoot myself: through the face or heart?"

It might be genetic, but it feels like I'm a stupid flouncy flower, destined to wilt at any second. I definitely didn't take that fact into account when I decided to dive in and create a multimillion-dollar entertainment company with absolutely no previous business experience.

Classic Felicia.

In 2011, Kim and I pitched YouTube the idea for a brand-new channel focusing on geek entertainment called Geek & Sundry. We went in armored with a bitchin' PowerPoint deck of all the cool shows we wanted to make. Even bought skirt suits to look official.

"Let's get in there and get us some funding!"

We high-fived like we were in some bro-comedy plotting to save our fraternity, then marched in to do businessing. And rocked our presentation.

Afterward, YouTube selected our channel as one of one hundred it would invest in. It was awesome. I mean, all those years of acting like a secretary in commercials was about to pay off in running my own company, right? Uh . . . kinda.

As much as I love creating things, the amount of work was, frankly crushing. As part of our deal with YouTube, we produced more than

420 videos in 2012 alone. More than sixty-two hours of content in a year. To put it in perspective, *The Guild* released *one and a half hours* of content in the same amount of time. A real television show releases ten to twenty-two hours a season. With a crew of up to a hundred to help.

We had eight full-time people. Total.

So the scale was . . . different.

But I hung on, like a tiny four-year-old grasping the curved bars of a playground merry-go-round when someone's older cousin spins it too fast. *YAY, THIS IS FUN, KINDA!* Then the months rolled along. And as time passed, I started to realize, *Holy crap. This "own-your-own-business" thing doesn't have an end point.*

The responsibilities of running a small company with huge ambitions shoved me squarely into areas I was not suited for. Like insurance liability coverage and an icky concept called "Management." Most of my time morphed from *making* things to *supervising* the making of said things. Kim and I had created *The Guild* by stretching ourselves as thin as possible to do everything. Perfect for a control freak like me. But in this new company, when I saw an employee doing something even slightly different than how I would have done it, I couldn't help it—I flipped.

"She used the wrong font? But the video is due to be uploaded in an hour! She's a North Korean spy sent to destroy us, isn't she?!"

It did NOT help that the skills I'd built up over the years didn't apply 100 percent to this new venture. Sometimes the opposite. Getting out from behind my computer and into people-meeting networking events was particularly jarring. Especially when it involved the advertising world, one of the places I had to spend a lot of time schmoozing, because it is the most backward, chauvinistic world I have ever encountered.

I'll never forget the time in Las Vegas when a supremely powerful ad exec I was encouraged to "get to know" looked me up and down as I approached and said, "Nice dress. I'd love to see it off you."

Um, hello. Nice to meet you, too?

When we launched Geek & Sundry on Sunday, April 1, 2012 (April Fool's Day, oh irony!), we did it with a day-long livestream "Subscribathon!" We invited tons of guests, held virtual panels, giveaways, dance competitions, you name it. We did anything we could to fill *twelve hours of programming*. I hosted the entire time, and at one point, in hour eight, I was so loopy I punched a unicorn in the face. Thank goodness the unicorn didn't sue.

The "Subscribathon!" was an excellent encapsulation of what that first year of running a business did to me.

On the outside, from 2012 through 2013, I was on top of the world. Privately, I collapsed completely. I was trying to juggle too much (running Geek & Sundry, maintaining an acting career, keeping up with the electric bill to keep my cats cool, and remembering to call my grandma EVER). And sure, the overwork contributed to it, but the real thing that made my world fall apart was the realization that season six of *The Guild*, which we produced with Geek & Sundry, needed to be the last.

The momentum of the show had stalled between moving from Xbox to YouTube. MMO video games and World of Warcraft had dipped in popularity. The show released months later than it should have because I didn't have the bandwidth to make it faster. All those factors impacted the fans. And views. Which in turn, made it hard to ask someone to fund a seventh season at a price point that had become unrealistic in the "Everyone has a web series in their garages now!" market.

The project had started to wind down.

Problem was, I had focused myopically on *The Guild* for six years. My work was my life. Conversations at parties I attended during those years went something like this:

"Hey, Felicia! Haven't seen you in a while!"

"Yeah, I've been working."

"You're the hardest-working person I know."

"I know!"

"Seen any movies?"

"No."

"Any TV?"

"Not really."

"Have you checked out my new web show?"

"No. But I'm finishing a new season of *The Guild*! It's great, Codex goes to—"

"Sorry to interrupt, I have to get a drink."

I understood. I thought I was a total bore, too.

Work-play balance is, in retrospect, something that can EASILY get out of whack. Especially if you're self-employed, you never turn it off. Your fate is in your own hands, so you can't let up. *Taking a weekend away for your birthday? Is your present to yourself RUINING YOUR LIFE?!* I don't think I could have achieved what I did with *The Guild* if I didn't have an insane-woman drive, but I made the mistake of transferring my self-worth wholly and completely. I was so excited that I'd found fulfilling work that I BECAME it. Felicia Day WAS *The Guild*.

There wasn't a day or night for six years where I wasn't obsessed with my show. *Let's see what people are thinking on Twitter. And Facebook and Tumblr. Then I'll check the forums. Yikes, we're due for another music video, better start writing. Damnit, I forgot to send out the newsletter. And did that contract for the DVD close yet? Why is the website down?!* On and on and on. When it looked like the show might end for good, you'd think I'd have been ecstatic. "Yeah! Mojitos for a year!" Instead, I panicked. Because I was facing a world where there'd be nothing of ME left.

That anxiety, plus the stress from working too hard on my start-up, pushed me to the edge of my own mind. I know that sounds after-school-special dramatic, but seriously, guys, I lost it. Big-time.

It wasn't the first time I'd struggled with depression and anxiety. At the height of *The Guild* success in 2010, after season three and our viral "Do You Wanna Date My Avatar" music video, I sat down to write the next season and cried for four months straight. The pressure of everyone's praise got to me. Not in a "Wow, they like what I did! Let's do more!" way, but in a "Wow, they like what I did. People are expecting great things now. I don't know what to give them to top it. Let me curl up and die now, please!" way.

I love it when people tell me I'm doing the wrong thing, or that something isn't possible, or just straight dismiss me. That lights my fire in a perverse way, like a two-year-old who deliberately touches the hot stove after you tell them not to. But compliment me or expect something big? That's the perfect way to destroy my confidence. There's a crazy people pleaser inside me screaming, *They won't like you if you mess up. You set the bar too high. They're all waiting for you to fail! And you're definitely going to. Good luck, stupidhead!*

I gave myself horrendous writer's block and almost ended the show because of my depression. Season four got written, but the ugly way, like too many layers of nail polish piled on top of each other. I'd start writing, then throw everything out and start from scratch. Over and over again. (Any writing book will tell you this is the WORST THING TO DO. I'll reinforce it here: don't do that.) Every time I'd get halfway through the script, I'd panic.

I don't know what Bladezz is doing here, I don't think the storyline makes sense. I'll have Codex get the job instead. But that breaks my whole outline. What do I do now? I don't have any ideas!

Commence three days of sobbing.

After a while, I was too paralyzed to decide anything at all. I woke up every single morning filled with dread, knowing I was going to have to sit down at my laptop and fail again. It's hard to understand how someone can get so incredibly depressed about the act of typing letters together, but I did it! That Stay Puft Marshmallow of Doom hovered over me for months. I destroyed a keyboard with my tears once. No joke: the left set of keys just stopped working. Okay, it was a combo of snot and tears and some Doritos dust, but same difference. Anxiety bled over into every aspect of my life (it wouldn't be the last time; hello, last Thursday!), and I had to be coaxed through the process by gentle and understanding friends.

Eventually, I got a version of the script done, and others around me helped me make it better. It wasn't pretty, it wasn't the best season, but we got through. And the year after, I wrote our fifth and BEST season in just ten days on vacation in Hawaii. So . . . that turned out better. (My inner muse loves them mai tais!)

Fast-forward three years, that same "You can't do it!" spirit returned with a vengeance. *Hey, are you feeling happy or confident? Let's fix that!* It was spring of 2012, in the middle of the Geek & Sundry launch, and amongst THAT storm of learning-curve ridiculousness, Kim and I were locked in months-long negotiations with *The Guild* cast to return the next season. I couldn't start writing the script with the possibility I would have to eliminate one of the main characters if one decided not to return. That put me, even before lifting my pen, into a state of panic.

"What do you mean we need to draft another version of the contract?"

"One of the cast's managers has a comment about the overtime provision."

"That will take another two weeks! Cancel the season, I don't want to write it."

"Felicia, calm down."

"I can't calm down! I have a script I haven't started that I need to finish! Give them whatever they want; I'll pay it out of my own pocket! Oh God, heart attack."

This attractive shrill tone in type has NOTHING on my attractive shrill tone in person. But I'd never learned how to deal with problems any differently. I grew up ruled by constant anxiety, and when my fears proved a tiny bit possible, even just a hint, I panicked and lashed out at myself and everyone around me. All in all, a real treat to work with! Many times, people in my life, including Kim and my *Guild* director Sean Becker, who headed most of the show after season one, tried to get me to enjoy the process of making the show, but underneath I couldn't let go of the idea that my dysfunctional anxiety was the REASON for our success. Like broody writers and their penchant for hard drinking. The idea that we could succeed without my obsessive problem-anticipating skills never sunk in. (To be super honest, I think I was just too proud to admit I had a problem. Denial is strong with this one.)

After two months of freaking out and bashing my head against the wall and pulling the plug on the season many times over, I finally found a theme in one of the guest characters I had created, Floyd Petrowski, a superstar game designer, who inspired me to write.

FLOYD

```
When I first started doing this, there were no
stakes, no pressure. I did it because I loved escap-
ing and creating things. Then we got successful and
people loved us. But now . . . it seems like they're
tired of what I do. And I can't think up anything
```

different enough for them to like me anymore. Total
failure-ville.

(DOESN'T SOUND PERSONAL AT ALL, RIGHT?!)

In the end, my character Codex helps him deal with his own anxiety and confronts his internet critics to remove what's blocking him in order to be able to create. Too bad I couldn't figure out how to write her into my own life, too.

Bit by bit, I stole enough time over the summer to write the script. But it wasn't fun. Instead of living the last creative days of my show with joy, they were filled with desperation. Because underneath it all, I knew the end was coming. I infused anxiety into every scene, like when I was hard-core into knitting and promised everyone I met I'd make them a scarf, even if I didn't like them. So I'd sit at home, knitting resentment and frustration into each row. "Why did I tell that random girlfriend of a colleague I'd make her a scarf out of CASHMERE?! I don't even know her last name!! Knit, hate, knit, hate, knit, hate!"

As we shot and edited the show, every episode we completed felt like a nail in the coffin of my career. The closer we got to completion, the larger the gaping mental chasm of "Who is Felicia Day after *The Guild* ends?" grew. Paranoid thoughts plagued me day and night.

I'll never make anything this good again.

Existence, what's up with that again?

I'd better breed and make babies, because I'm getting old and my uterus is drying up like the Sahara.

It didn't make me fun to be around or work with. I needed to take a long break to find myself again, but with Geek & Sundry going a thousand miles per hour, I couldn't make the train stop even for a second. I was trained to get an A in life from everyone, so I never learned how to take care of myself even if I had a right to.

"I'm recovering from an operation, but yes, I can appear in your web series for free! Please like me!"

The pressure just got more and more intense, from myself and from the world. And in the spring of 2013, a few months after *The Guild* finished, when I was restructuring the company and still working eighteen hours a day nonstop, my problems got serious.

Stress started killing me. Literally.

I developed severe panic attacks in the middle of the night. At 4:30 a.m. on the dot, I'd wake up with my heart pounding in my chest, like someone was standing over me with a butcher knife, trying to kill me in my sleep. (There was never anyone there, FYI.) I'd lie there panicking about the show's end, my business, internet comments, yelling at people in my head until I fretted myself to sleep again. Every night for *months*.

During the day, I became frantic to find a way to validate myself again. I started five different new projects, then abandoned them just as quickly because I couldn't get them done *immediately* to show people and get external praise. I became more and more desperate to make Geek & Sundry a bigger success. This put pressure on everyone around me in the company, especially since I started planning ridiculously far ahead, alert to every random disaster scenario possible.

"Do we have a backup system in place in triplicate for our videos? What's going to happen when the big earthquake hits in 2048? Will we have master copies of our web shows in storage?! Commence emergency protocol, go go go!!"

My fear of the future became paralyzing. It strained my relationship with Kim, my business partner of six years and probably contributed to her leaving our company, one of my biggest regrets. That ended one of the most wonderful, artistically rewarding relationships of my life.

Keep reading, it gets worse!

My moods were reliable—in that they were consistently, AB-SOLUTELY INSANE. They'd roller coaster so far and fast day to day, hour to hour <happy SAD motivated DEPRESSED angry MANIC!!!>. My warped and anxious state of mind spiraled tighter and tighter, compressing to the point where I lost my memory. Completely, like a character with amnesia in a pulp detective novel. Romantic? Not so much. I literally couldn't remember things from my childhood, people's names, even simple things like, "What's the name of the redhead actor in *Harry Potter*?" Things I KNEW that I knew! (Rupert Grint, sorry, pal. I'll never forget you again.) The sheer act of *thinking* felt like sloughing through thick molasses. I couldn't trust my own mind anymore, which was the scariest thing I've ever experienced. Once, I stared at a plate of food for fifteen minutes, unable to figure out if I liked green beans or not. I honestly couldn't remember. To be unsure of what you like, what you feel, who you are? Believe me, it's utterly terrifying.

During all of this I continued to appear at conventions and conferences around the world, making speeches and doing panels and signing autographs. Which you'd think would make me feel better. People enjoying my work seems like a nice ego boost? Nope, I dodged those bullets of hope like a pessimist pro! The appearances actually made all my impostor feelings even worse. I would sob before going out to meet people because I felt like such a fraud. I didn't deserve their compliments. *Why do they want to talk about my work? It's all in the past. Months old. Can't they see what a worthless piece of crap I am now?*

In my warped state of mind, I had nothing new to offer my fans and I probably wouldn't ever again. I deserved to be hated, not loved.

These were the worst days of my life.

In retrospect, crappy chemicals in my brain were working overtime, driving me to destroy myself, like that thing that makes lemmings throw themselves over a cliff. (That's actually folklore based on a Disney documentary where the filmmakers in the 1960s flung lemmings over the edge of the cliff for their movie. Horrible. But the video game was awesome, amiright?)

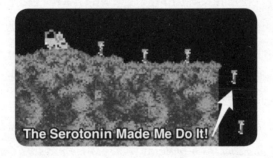

The Serotonin Made Me Do It!

I tried superficial things to control my world, like losing weight, but that just left me gaunt and freezing all the time. I'd lie in bed and feel my bones, aware of how much closer my skeleton was to the sheets. It felt . . . good. In a twisted and perverse and self-destructive way. If I couldn't control my life, I could control THIS, however bad it was for me in the end.

Luckily, I forced myself out of that phase, because internet commenters started typing beneath my videos, "Felicia has old face now." Thanks, trolls. You did something good for once!

I developed an irrational hatred toward anything around me that was familiar. My bedroom curtains, the collar my dog wore, my car seats. (I suddenly HATED tan. Or did I?) I felt nauseated and trapped by every single object and person around me. *If I wake up one more day and see that* Princess Bride *poster on my wall, I'm gonna take a sledgehammer to it. It's trapping me here. I'm going to die looking at it. STOP OPPRESSING ME, POSTER!*

From people close to me, to the way my desk was organized, every detail represented being frozen in a situation I couldn't escape: my life.

At the lowest point (among some champion lows, I might add), I started fantasizing about deleting my Twitter account and erasing myself from the internet. It escalated to constant daydreams about disappearing entirely. Meaning . . . dying. My musings revolved around scenarios of how I could end myself. I don't think I ever got to the point where I was serious about going through with my plans, but I was obsessed with thinking about them. I learned later that there's a term for this: "suicidal ideation."

I wonder how people would react to me doing a backflip off a cliff during this photo shoot? Or walking out into Comic-Con traffic? Or electrocuting myself with a gaming console in a French claw-foot bathtub? That would make a cool crime scene photo.

Would anyone vlog about it?

And at that point, when things got THAT weird in my head . . .

. . . I still didn't get help.

[Heal It Up, Woman.]

After a summer of mental problems in 2013, I got *physically* sick for two months straight. And my boyfriend finally muscled me into doing something about it.

"You have to see a doctor."

"I'm fine."

"You can't sleep. You walk around in a haze, and you cough all the time. I think you might be turning into a zombie."

"I'm FINE."

"You look super tired in your videos lately. Eye bags and stuff."

LONG MINUTE of silence. "Calling someone right now."

It's true, it had been a year since I felt energetic, healthy, or normal. Depression can do that, but . . . could there be something else?

Guess what I discovered when I finally made a doctor's appointment after procrastination for another few months? There were actual REASONS I was sick. And some of them affected my brain area. Experts can know stuff sometimes!

I discovered that I had an extremely severe thyroid problem that was causing a lot of my depression and lack of energy and was probably the reason my hair had fallen out in chunks over the summer. (Led to a snappy-ass haircut, though!) I also discovered huge awful fibroids in my lady parts that were gunking up the works and had to be removed, and BEST PART, at the end of 2013, as a Christmas present of sorts, I discovered that my acid reflux had gotten so bad because of stress that I'd developed a thing called Barrett's esophagus. (It's usually a condition only old dudes in their fifties get.) The lining of my stomach was creeping up my throat and converting all the good tissue to bad tissue, and because of this problem, I was a thousand times more likely to get esophageal cancer than the rest of the population at large, which . . .

WAIT.

WHAT THE FUCK?!

And THAT is when I decided to get control of my life back. Because for some reason, I didn't merit it worthy enough to take extreme action when my *mind* got sick. But my *body*? Emergency timez!

Imagine saying to someone, "I have a kidney problem, and I'm having a lot of bad days lately." Nothing but sympathy, right?

"What's wrong?"

"My mom had that!"

"Text me a pic of the ultrasound!"

Then pretend to say, "I have severe depression and anxiety, and I'm having a lot of bad days lately."

They just look at you like you're broken, right? Unfixable. Inherently flawed. Maybe not someone they want to hang around as much?

Yeah, society sucks.

My mental problems made me feel ashamed. I felt like I had to hide them until I could "work through it" on my own. Which I never did, because I didn't know how. And I didn't feel brave enough to make fixing my mind a priority because I didn't think anyone would understand. Having an increased chance for cancer, though? I'm too neurotic NOT to be a hypochondriac. So damn, did I get ruthless!

I said "NO!" to everything. A very good friend of mine told me once, "Of everyone I know, you need to build a bubble around yourself." Well, I took steps to inflate that bubble. Anything that gave me the remotest iota of stress, I dumped. I set extreme parameters around my company. "I'll be working from home now. I'm only coming into the Geek & Sundry office once a week, and if I don't feel like doing that, I won't."

"How long?"

"However long I need."

Once you tell people exactly what you will and won't do, it's amazing how they'll adjust. Or they won't. And then an opportunity or relationship goes away. And that's okay.

Once I got my body on the right track, slowly but surely healing, day by day, I started working to repair my mind. It was not easy, because everything felt shattered into a thousand-piece puzzle. But I finally sat down and tried to put those pieces back together, one by one.

I started with months of self-involved and semi-crazed journaling. I filled five notebooks with every insecurity and rage and sadness I could think of. I wrote down everything I felt, including terrible things about people I loved, in order to move through and get to the TRUTH of what I couldn't see through my fogged state of mind. And I hate to say it, but the more ruthless I got, the better I felt.

"I hate X's face! I've hated him for years!"

Working through my initial reaction always got me to understand what was really going on.

"Okay, I don't really *hate* him. I really feel upset about that one time he forgot to invite me to his birthday party. I mean, everyone we knew was posting so many fun Instagram pictures, and I pressed a heart on all of them even though the whole time I was curled up in my bed sobbing!"

Also, deeper and less funny stuff than that.

I dug and dug and kept digging. All that introspection helped me get perspective and realize, *This thing I'm feeling, it might NOT be the TRUTH* . . .

There's a great Eleanor Roosevelt quote, "No one can make you feel inferior without your consent." Well, I discovered that, even though the feeling had ruled me my entire life, no one could make me be *anxious* without my consent. It was an amazing realization.

And yes, I did seek professional mental help. But avoidant habits die hard. So instead of going directly to a certified specialist, first I decided to try the softball approach and hired a "creativity life coach." Boy, did this woman embrace the clichés of her profession *hard*. She wore a lot of tie-dye. I had to carry crystals to "ward off the negative spirits." Just entering her office every week gave my sinus cavities aromatherapy seizures. Oh, and she loved the hypnosis.

"You are a tree. You are the trunk. You have to cut off the branches that are draining you and concentrate on that part before you can reach outside yourself again. Repeat after me, I am a trunk."

"I feel stupid, but I am a trunk. I am a trunk."

Talking to a real objective human who was a captive audience (since I was paying her) was a good first step. But when she wanted to move on to some strange rebirth regression therapy with screaming and stuff, it occurred to me that she wasn't accredited and could legally blog about how weird I was later. So FINALLY I moved on and got my very own certified psychologist. With a lying-down couch and everything!

Showing up each week and having someone to complain to without the fear of someone tweeting about it was <u>spectacular</u>. I would recommend ANYONE try it. We're all a garbage dump of dysfunction, but if you get in there and churn the problems, they turn to mulch faster so new things can grow out of them. (I have no idea how to mulch, so I hope that analogy is accurate.)

Even with all those efforts, recovery was slow. A few months in, I was ready to give myself an Olympic gold medal for minuscule things. Like mustering the effort to refill an empty toilet paper roll. *Look at you taking initiative. Go, girl!*

But after a while, and I mean MONTHS of learning how to be a real human and attending several new-wave '80s concerts (hearing "The Safety Dance" in person can be incredibly healing), the pressure I'd put on myself my whole life . . . lightened. Eventually, I emerged from my own private Hades. And I used the time to re-form my brain to be less anxious, live in the present, and not panic about the future or regret the past. (As much as I could, having installed so much messed-up hard-wiring before.)

I started getting creative ideas for the company again. I got motivated to throw out my old stretched-out bras that hung open at the top like a pocket. During that time of self-care, I became a different person. But it was fine. Everyone adjusted to the "new me," including me.

Eleven months later, during the summer of 2014, I was eating a burrito in my car before a Geek & Sundry meeting I was super excited about. I thought about all the people in my life who'd helped me through the horrible year and a half before, and realized, *Wow, it must have been really hard on my boyfriend/business partner/friends for me to be so unhappy for so long.* And I started crying. Because it felt like I had finally recovered enough to be able to think about other people again. (There was also a Mumford & Sons song playing at the time. Banjo + Black Beans = Waterworks.)

Yeah, yeah, success is a ladder, a marathon instead of a sprint and all that crap. Everyone can TELL you stuff like that, but you really have to understand advice in relation to YOURSELF, or it's all just nice intellectual theory.

Weathering the rough times requires a lot of self-confidence outside the things you can't control, like career and what other people think of you. You need to be able to feel proud of yourself even if you were living in a tiny hut in the middle of nowhere, taking care of goats. You are unique and good enough JUST AS YOU ARE. As a theoretical goat herder.

It was the toughest lesson of my life, learning how to let *The Guild* go. And how to manage a business bigger than a one-garage web show. Even tougher than the forty-man raids in World of Warcraft. I have many new projects with my company and outside it that I care about now, but none of them will ever be all of me. I learned better than to let that crap happen again.

In the end, I'm able to look back without shame or regretful nostalgia, and think, *You made something great. And something new will come around. Or not. Either way, do the work you love. And love yourself. That's all you can do in this world in order to be happy.*

#GamerGate
and Meeeeee!

> That one time when having a vagina and a love
> of video games was not such a great combo.

I have a folder labeled "Hate Folder" that sits in the middle of my desktop. It's where I save screenshots of the worst things people have said to me online. ("Fifty Shades of Felicia!") For some reason, it takes the sting away to herd all the toxic comments into a corner of my hard drive, aggregating the losers I'd like to hunt down in real life and run over with a dump truck.

Then back up, and run over again! (Too far?)

If it's too disgusting to say to another human being, I guarantee someone has said it to me online. The internet is amazing because it connects us with one another. But it's also horrific because . . . it connects us with one another. Whether we want the connection or not. The only real-life analogy I can think of is if a random person were allowed to walk into your home, punch you in the face while you're eating your oatmeal, then walk out again with no fear of consequences. After one incident you'd be looking for a new zip code, huh?

Here are some fun examples of the human awfulness I've collected over the years.

@feliciaday A Woman using sexuality to profit from male gamers and pretending she's empowering women and progressing "gaming culture".

her nose is so fucked up.

did someone go at it with a sledgehammer or what

@feliciaday congratulations you have a vagina and play video games, now do something useful

if you honestly think **Felicia Day** worked hard to get where she is, eat a bowl of fucking nails

Why do gamer girls always use the terms Nerd, Geek and Gamer? Can't Felicia Day just shut the fuck up? She is nothing but an attention whore that uses her gender has a key for attention.
Tell me, would you be subscribed to this channel if Felicia Day wasn't a girl? If you say yes, then you're a fucking idiot.

someone tell that red headed cunt, that the kitchen is down the hall and not in front of the camera.

Once someone posts that you're "So ugly I wouldn't have sex with your corpse," that's when you know you've arrived online!

And sure, everyone says the best approach to negative comments is "Don't feed the trolls," that ignoring negativity is the best policy. This approach is great in theory, but emotionally, it's *HUMANLY IMPOSSIBLE*.

Biology backs me up. It's proven that our brains give more attention to negative experiences than positive ones. (I read it in a study. Reference: internet.) Every online creator jokes about how you can read a thousand great comments about your work, but it's always a single terrible one that makes you think, *They're right. I should be ejected into the vacuum of space. It would be a public service.* REASON: One of the brain's main jobs is to alert us to environmental threats. That's probably why I have a "Hate Folder" rather than a "You're Awesome" folder. (Note from inner therapist: start one of those.) Over the years, I thought I'd seen it all. I thought I'd experienced every rotten thing the internet could fling at people.

And then #GamerGate happened. A perfect, hateful, digital

gumbo that gave the gaming world, and me, a black eye not soon to be healed.

I'll summarize the history briefly for anyone out of the loop. From my point of view. Because it's my book. If you illegally downloaded this chapter just to parse and argue with my interpretation of events line by line (and I know it will happen, yay!), well, you're probably the kind of person I'm not very nice to in this section anyway.

Hello! Not a pleasure to meet you!

The whole #GamerGate thing started in August 2014, with a guy getting revenge over a really bad breakup by publishing every excruciatingly and maniacally specific detail online.

I found out about it early on, after seeing a bunch of gamers I follow on Twitter talking about "that Zoe post." *Oooh, gossip? I'm at home on a Friday night wearing sweats and eating cheddar popcorn as usual. Juicy!* I clicked over to read a long, rambling blog entry, scrolled down page after page to see IMs, emails, and other private information a guy had collected on his ex-girlfriend and published for the world to rummage through. Evidence of her cheating on him, peppered with implications of sexual favors traded for reviews of the game Depression Quest that she had designed (accusations that were later disproven. Repeat: disproven). It was creepy. I remember being horrified. Then judging her a little. Then feeling bad about it. And then thinking, *What woman would ever date this creep again?!*

Usually controversy, even this terrible, disappears pretty fast on the internet. The people whose hobby it is to hate things move on to rip apart a new game or make fun of a celebrity's vacation cellulite. But this situation started, strangely, to gather more and more steam. More hatred and, most frightening: a strange sense of *justice* on the part of the attackers. I think the same viral effect that leads people to share a crazy Korean music video a billion times is the same kind of phenomenon that helped give rise to #GamerGate. You can FEEL the wave of emotion online when something is about to go viral, good or bad. A scientist I met once mathematically compared internet behavior to swarm behavior seen in starlings or locusts. Well, that weekend, the hate locusts started swarming.

Hackers leaked Zoe's personal information. She received rape and death threats and was forced from her home. Videos of her nude photos were spread and Photoshopped across the internet to shame her, much to the amusement of the trolls. People even tracked down her father to call him and tell him what a "whore your daughter is." (I mean, how sad do you have to be as a human to think THAT was a good use of your afternoon?)

As someone who has been an advocate in gaming for many years, especially as a woman, I watched all this happen from the sidelines and thought, *This is disgusting!* I wanted to step up and speak up against the bullying . . . but I didn't. Why?

Because I was afraid. On a much smaller scale, I'd been on the receiving end of a slice of this hate myself. And I didn't want to relive any part of it.

The roots of both incidents lie in 4chan, an anonymous website generally associated with hate speech and cartoon porn addiction, and the starting point for the attacks on Zoe Quinn. Basically, it's the watercooler for some of the worst of the internet.

In 2012, after all my years on the web, I thought I'd developed some pretty tough troll armor until some people on 4chan decided to attack me en masse for a music video I did for my weekly Geek & Sundry web show, *The Flog*. My friend Jason Miller is a country music artist, and at the time I thought it would be fun to combine his style with my love of gaming and see what happened. Okay, SURE, nature probably didn't want those two things mashed together EVER, but that was the point of the show: to throw things against the wall and see if they stuck. I wanted to sing and be creative and hoped the audience would enjoy the experience as much as I did!

Oh, you naïve, dumb-ass girl.

We spent a few hundred dollars to make the video, borrowed someone's house, and shot in the desert without a fire permit. We didn't light any matches, so it was cool. The end result was cute. Not mind-blowing, but the song was well produced, and I got to dress up as *Tomb Raider* character Lara Croft, which was a bucket list item. (And proved to me that big boobs DO look better in tank tops. I stuffed HARD.)

I uploaded it like any other video, with the attitude, *It's free to watch! Don't dig it? No harm, no foul, right?* Er . . . not so much.

Contempt for women who call themselves "Gamer Girls" has existed for a while online. In fact, I'd been careful to avoid the label over the years for that very reason. But I decided to title the video "Gamer Girl, Country Boy" anyway. And that gave the people who hated me, and who hated the very concept of women having a voice in gaming, a reason to attack. And their feedback was awesome!

Country Music: Trigger Genre

The video was shared on a 4chan forum and a tidal wave of bile hit the video. Hundreds and hundreds of comments, the depravity of which even jaded little me had never seen.

I was talentless. I was fake and hideous and ugly. (I'll admit I'd made a bright yellow eye shadow choice that I'll rue until the day I'm dead.) I was denigrated on every personal level, my work dismissed as the desperate and pathetic attempts of an "attention whore." According to the comments, I got where I was by manipulating geeks with my looks, and at the same time, I was repulsively ugly and hard to masturbate to. As a crowning achievement, I was deemed responsible for the "downfall of gaming."

A multibillion-dollar industry destroyed by little ol' me? Aw, shucks!

Anyone who defended me online was called a "white knight neckbeard," a term that describes a guy who defends a girl online solely in order to get laid. A lot of the time, it works. And if you were a *woman* defending me, pish, you weren't even worth addressing. Hateful, bullying comments flooded the supportive community I was so proud of creating. Even my most hard-core fans were left reeling.

I certainly was.

After about ten thousand misogynistic and a ton of FACTUALLY INACCURATE comments (trash me if you will, but do a little research first), they finally got to me. I'd been making videos for five years at that point. I've seen animated GIFs of myself doing . . . you don't wanna know. Some involving very forward dolphins.

The comments spread like a fungus across my self-confidence. It devastated me to see people dismiss my career because of one four-minute video. I felt ashamed for creating it and everything else I'd ever made. I thought, *Is this what people have been thinking for years? How stupid was I to think I could sing? I don't want to be SEEN ever again.*

For months I stopped putting my heart into the things I made. It was one of the reasons I couldn't write the last *Guild* season without feeling crippling self-doubt on every page.

Sad but true, I did what I have told so many people over and over not to do:

I let the trolls get to me.

I didn't realize at the time how much that incident affected me, but I stepped away from gaming in a lot of subtle ways. I still considered myself part of the world, but I turned down a ton of jobs and event appearances. And those changes in my behavior all led me to stifle myself when I felt the urge to speak up about #GamerGate.

The timing was particularly bad, personally, because a few weeks into the uproar, at the end of August 2014, the infamous "Celebrity Hacking Scandal" happened, where dozens of prominent actresses and performers had private nude pictures stolen and exposed to the world. (Wow, jerks were really busy that fall ruining lives online! Also: the stolen pictures were first posted on 4chan. So much great stuff originates there, huh?)

As someone nowhere NEAR the victims on the celebrity-importance ladder, imagine my surprise when I was contacted by several hackers via my HACKED phone number warning me that I was a future target. My name was on a request list for compromising photos, and people were supposedly offering big dollars to back it up. I counted myself lucky that I had fans in the hacker world. (How cool, right?) But being hunted for boobies? Slightly terrifying.

So, while Zoe and other people were being ripped apart online,

I was holding my tongue, trying to erase anything from my online accounts that I didn't want made public for the world to see. Any picture, *Is that too much side boob? I'll erase it.* Any email, *OMG why would I think that was funny?! Delete.* I spent a week ripping out pieces of my digital life that I didn't want people poking around. I'm sure I missed a lot. When you examine your underwear close enough, EVERYTHING looks a little bit suspect.

I knew sharing my thoughts about the situation would burn me. So I stayed out. And with other prominent people, men and women, jumping in to take a stand against the bullying and hatred, I honestly thought the whole thing would go away soon. I think everyone sane in the gaming world did.

But it didn't. It got worse. Because the issue somehow morphed from attacking a single woman over a messed-up revenge post to a quasi-conservative movement striving for "ethics in game journalism." A large segment of the newly anointed "#GamerGate movement" decided that as a result of "the Zoe post" there was corruption running rampant in the game journalism world. And THEY were the people to fix it.

They focused a large amount of their wrath on people trying to add dialogue about feminism and diversity in gaming, condemning them as "Social Justice Warriors." (That label was always so weird to me, because how is that an insult? "Social Justice Warrior" actually sounds pretty badass.) It turned into a mob. One that was disjointed, with lots of differing agendas, but all surfing the wave of vengeful emotion together. Like the French Revolution over that cake thing.

The attacks grew way beyond Zoe. Friends in the indie games

industry who stepped up to defend her started receiving the same treatment. Verbally harassed. Doxxed (where someone hacks personal information like phone number, address, credit cards, social security number and posts it online for the whole world to see and misuse, super awesome experience). At the same time, a prominent vlogger named Anita Sarkeesian released an installment of her video series examining feminist issues in gaming. Hatred of her in a certain demographic of the internet, I'm pretty sure a one-to-one with the worst of the attackers, only fed the "You're trying to ruin my gaming!" frenzy. More and more people in gaming who started speaking up, especially women, were mobbed for it. A journalist named Jenn Frank wrote a piece about the attacks on Zoe and was so badly swarmed with hate that she decided to quit the industry. I dipped my toe in the water once and sent one subtle @ tweet to Jenn in support and received so many hateful comments I had to log offline for two days. Great "ethical" achievements there, guys!

Ironically, the #GamerGate movement never focused on some of the big game companies who actually ARE unethical, bribing vloggers and censoring bad reviews on their products. The movement tended to target smaller journalists and independent gaming sites. Mostly the ones who were criticizing THEM. It was mind-boggling, but at the same time, they did create the biggest movement in gaming history. And it seemed like it would never stop growing.

At the end of October, I flew to Vancouver to work on the TV show *Supernatural*. It was more than two months after the initial blog post (a decade in real-life time), and the gaming world was STILL drowning in #GamerGate. I was walking down the street on one of my days off and saw two gamer guys walking toward me in classic, black crew-neck gaming T-shirts. One Call of Duty, the other Halo.

Now, in the past, whenever I saw another gamer in public, I would feel heartened, because we *belonged* no matter if we stopped to chat or not. I would go out of my way to exchange a knowing glance, a supportive smile signaling, *Yeah, dude. It's cool that you game. I do, too!* We were automatically compatriots in our love for something we both knew was awesome.

But as those two gamers walked toward me, for the first time in my life I didn't have the impulse to say hello. Or smile. For some reason as I approached the corner . . . I crossed the street instead.

I sat down a few blocks later, because I couldn't understand what I'd just done. Then I realized that because of the recent situation with #GamerGate, subconsciously I no longer assumed that a random gamer and I would be on the same page, or would connect just because of our love of gaming. There was a wedge in my world where there had been none before.

And for the first time in months . . . I got angry. I WANTED TO WRITE SOME SHIT DOWN, SON!

I pounded five espresso shots, ran back to my hotel room, and wrote a Tumblr post about my experience titled, "Crossing the Street." And I tried to make it different from the tone of other writing on the subject. I tried to frame my argument in an empathetic way. Not condemn, but make people understand what I was feeling. How I was upset and ashamed at my impulse to avoid those anonymous gamers. How sad I was that the actions of #GamerGate had created that feeling in me, to separate myself from people whom I would have assumed were comrades before. And how the whole situation was creating the outside impression of a culture driven by misogyny and hatred, which I KNEW wasn't true. I appealed to our mutual love of gaming, on both sides, to bring us back together, for the sake of what we all loved. (The essay was eloquent, promise. Legal drugs fuel good words!)

I emphasized my fear of speaking out, because of the possibility that someone would doxx me. I had taken out too many restraining orders against stalkers to not be concerned about my home address leaking. I thought sharing that fear would be the "Relatable!" part to both sides. I mean, anyone would be afraid if it was easy for a whackadoodle to pull up into their driveway when they got angry at one of your tweets, right? "I'm the owner of that taco place you just dissed. WATCH OUT, I'M ON YOUR DOORSTEP, BITCH!"

I posted my essay on Tumblr minutes before I had to hop in the car to go to the movie studio that night, and as I hit Send, I felt dizzy with hubris. I'm not brave in general—*mousey* doesn't just describe my real hair color—but speaking out felt RIGHT. It was something that I should have done weeks before. By overcoming my fear, I had finally redeemed myself TO myself. No matter if anyone paid attention or not.

I got in the car to be driven to set for work (they do that on TV shows, so fancy). Twenty minutes later I got a call. I looked at the caller ID. "Wil Wheaton." That was weird. We're super-close friends, we've acted together, we produce a web show together, but it was odd he was calling me. Email/text/IM/Twitter/Snapchat? Yes. Primitive old-school telephoning? Nope.

"Hello?"

"Dude, you need to disable comments on your Tumblr post." He sounded panicked.

"What?"

"Several people have posted your home address in the comments. You need to disable comments right now."

"Oh my God."

I was silent for a second. Then I learned that "bathed in horror" is an actual feeling, not a colorful writing metaphor.

"But . . . I . . . don't know . . . I don't know my password."

I had just changed everything to forty-character twelve-step identification the week before because of the celebrity hacking thing, and I hadn't reentered any of my passwords onto my phone yet. It was one of those "That sucks!" coincidences.

"Do you want me to reset it for you? I'm not home but I can find some Wi-Fi."

"No . . . then you'd have to get in my email, and I don't know that password, either. Wait, maybe I can do it on my phone. I'll call you back."

I hung up and tried to load the Tumblr app, but discovered the interface was not easy to navigate when your hands are trembling in an aggressive way. The driver, a very kind older guy, offered to pull the car over.

"No . . . no, I don't want to be . . . late for work." My voice was as unsteady as my hands as I fumbled with the phone.

Within a few minutes I got my password reset. Only to discover that I couldn't disable the comments plug-in from my phone. Crap.

At that point I started hyperventilating. All I could picture was awful people storming my house while I was out of town and killing my dog. Totally irrational, I know. But he was very old and friendly and the perfect target for malicious intent.

I knew the longer my address was up, the more it would be shared and stored and available to anyone forever, bad or good.

In my heart, I knew it was too late to prevent that anyway.

I finally contacted a friend who disabled the comments on the post. (Which I will never turn on again, forever and ever and ever, yay!) There were more than a thousand comments in the thread at that point, a lot of them vile and antagonistic and awful, exactly what you WOULDN'T expect as a reaction to an essay with the theme, *Let's hold hands and get through this, guys!* But such was the level of vitriol at the time. Oh, and there were also four separate people who posted my address with malicious intent. A few were business addresses and a few were definitely NOT.

In the scene we filmed that night, my character, Charlie, murdered someone on-screen. The experience was more than a little cathartic.

I'll leave the analysis of why #GamerGate happened, what drove it, and why it lasted as long as it did to someone's kick-ass graduate thesis. (Hope you get an A!) But hostility to outside criticism has long been a weirdly accepted part of gaming culture. You don't generally see hard-core knitters reply to someone who says, "Knitting is cool, but the needles could be made from more environmentally sustainable wood," with "Oh no you don't, idiot. My knitting is perfect the way it is, don't you DARE try to change it. You're obviously a fake. What's the diameter of that yarn? Don't know? Go die in a fire!"

The mainstream media was already publishing "What the hell is going on in the nerd world?" articles about #GamerGate and quickly picked up on my story. "Felicia Day's Fears Come True" became the headline of the week, mostly emphasizing the violation of my personal information, because, you know, that was the sexy part. The *Guardian*, *Time*, the *Washington Post*—even the *New York Times*—all reported on my doxxing. Most of the gaming and online community showed an amazing amount of support. But, to me, the reaction of #GamerGate itself was the most fascinating.

In the initial comments section of my Tumblr post, which I disabled, there are hundreds of condescending, hateful comments attacking me as a woman, labeling me a weakling and a fake gamer.

Who liked Felicia Day though?

I feel bad for her. It must be terrible to go through life being that retarded.

Yeah, I remember her with longer hair in Eureka now.
She is past her prime now.

she's a nobody.

Her words are as barren as her womb.

funny, when push comes to shove all these stuck up bitches who claim to have geek cred will show just how much they loathe us "nerds"
as long as it made her look cool she was a gamer now that its not hip to be seen with us she crosses the street.

Scared of gamers in the street, jesus fucking christ just don't fucking breed woman spare future generations your spastic seed.

Felicia you made your bed, now sleep in it.

One of the top discussion points in #GamerGate forums was about how I "wasn't really doxxed." Some claimed I did it myself for publicity (?!) or qualified it as inconsequential because the information wasn't hard enough to obtain.

Just to clear the record, it is true to say I wasn't doxxed in the exact way that the other victims of #GamerGate were. I was "lucky." Because (and I've never said this publicly, but hell, let's just tell-it-all, baby!) I'd been doxxed by 4chan already, the year before.

In 2013, a group on that forum tracked down a ton of personal information on me. They shared all that and pictures of the outside of my house and my license plate amongst themselves. A disturbed fan used that information and showed up at my front door, made his way INTO MY HOUSE, and afterward, proceeded to obsess over me online in an erratic and abusive way to the extent that I was terrified he would show up again and do something violent.

So that's why so many haters were able to post my address so quickly a year later. Efficient, huh?

The savviest members of #GamerGate saw all the media coverage blowing up over my situation and decided that my doxxing was making them look bad, so they rushed to send me well wishes of support on Twitter. But the support was almost always accompanied with the caveat: "REAL #GamerGate doesn't do stuff like this."

This was the part that was the hardest for me to understand. Because whether the people who did the actual act were in the group or not was beside the point.

#GamerGate as a movement created an environment for attacks to flourish. Hell, it <u>ORIGINATED</u> with them. A great quote from a video series called *Folding Ideas* put it best: "The use of fear tactics, even if only by a minority, creates an environment of fear that all members enjoy the privilege of, whether they engage in them or not." This was the very reason I felt afraid to speak up in the first place. And what I feared most? Yeah, it happened. In light of that fact, the qualified apologies felt hollow at best. Especially when, for every nice comment from #GamerGate, I saw dozens of comments like the following.

> @feliciaday
> Feminists call anything they dislike scary bc they know it triggers white knights #GamerGate

> @feliciaday Felicia could have supported #gamergate and became a hero. But she took the SJW shill route and paid the price.

> @feliciaday It's a pity she chose the wrong side and became part of the problem. Gamergate isn't about misogyny.

> @feliciaday your stance in favor of bullying, hate, and nerd shaming is deeply disappointing. you've lost a fan. for life. #gamergate

> @feliciaday We just want an end to corruption. It just so happens that some of the people corrupt are women and feminists.

> @feliciaday I know it hurts, but what Felicia Day did was a pr hitpiece. She's part of the media too.

> @feliciaday @GeekandSundry i hope you die

It took six months for me to become comfortable with walking my dog at night (*Let's be crazy tonight, Cubby, and not carry mace!*), and I will never feel 100 percent safe in my own home again. I have had people sitting in cars outside my window, certified letters sent to my address just to say "I know where you live," and phone calls from strange area codes at all hours of the night. Now that I know how easy it is for anyone with an agenda to track me down, feeling safe is a cute, nostalgic feeling.

What frightened me the most about my #GamerGate experience was the possibility that this could be the future of the internet. That the utopia I thought the online world created, where people don't have to be ashamed of what they love and could connect with each other regardless of what they looked like, was really a place where people could steep themselves in their own worldview until they became willfully blind to everyone else's.

I guess the internet can be both things. Good and bad. And I have been "lucky" enough to experience the crazy extremes of both.

I had to think long and hard about writing this chapter, and I know there's a good chance I will have more of my privacy violated as a result. There will certainly be another flood of online attacks because of it.

So after all that, would I speak up again?

Absolutely.

Because shame is a very good barometer. The very reason I felt guilty about NOT speaking up is WHY I should have spoken up in the first place.

All that is necessary for the triumph of evil
is that good men do nothing.
EDMUND BURKE (1729-1797)
(OR MAYBE NOT, ACCORDING TO WIKIPEDIA)

I recently got a message from a mother who said, "I asked my fourteen-year-old what #GamerGate was and he said, 'It's because women are trying to ruin video games.'" I was so upset. Unless people are speaking out to counteract that idea, how will that kid ever think differently?

Over the years, I've heard many times that *The Guild* and what I do online got them into gaming and web video. I'm proud to be able to represent something, however small, to some people. Because, in my own experience, sometimes a little representation is all it takes to inspire people to follow a path they never would have considered.

As a middle-school-aged kid, I fell in love with the fact that Nora Ephron, a woman, wrote and directed *Sleepless in Seattle*. It was my absolute favorite movie, and I watched it enough times to destroy the copy I had on VHS. (I don't know how many times that is, but typing that just now made me feel old, like someone in the 1960s waxing nostalgic about their Victrola.)

Everything about that movie was amazing. The romance, the miscommunications, the idea that I was destined to have baby-making times with Tom Hanks. And while I watched, time and time again, I had this vague sense of a puppeteer figure behind the scenes. A person who was responsible for building a world I wanted to be a part of SO BADLY. She was unseen, but her hand was in every detail. Emphasis on *HER*.

I cried when Nora Ephron died in 2012, which was bizarre to me at the time. Usually when a celebrity dies I think, *Oh, that's sad*, then get irritated when their name trends on Twitter (because sometimes they AREN'T dead, and then I feel like a jerk for assuming anyone over forty is ready to swan dive into a crematorium). I never met her in person. I never had a poster of her on my wall or sent letters to her fan club (like I did with Richard Grieco; YES, that happened), but with her death, a little bit of my childhood inspiration disappeared. She had made it possible for me to imagine my own future in the world of film. Her very existence showed me it could be done and allowed me to dream about following the path she laid behind her. Without her work, I doubt it would have ever occurred to me that such a path existed.

Now, I certainly am not saying that I consider myself an icon like Nora Ephron or that I should be held up as the world's ultimate example of "GAMER FEMALE!" but the idea of representation is important. And I think the world of gaming needs people from all walks of life to speak up and represent the positive side of what we love. Because, let's be real: gaming's reputation is NOT good in that area right now. Currently, if it were a restaurant, it would get a VERY bad Yelp review.

 Felicia D.
Los Angeles, CA
9 friends
9 reviews

    2/16/2014

1 check-in here

I loved the food at this establishment but as soon as I entered, the atmosphere felt a tad unfriendly. A few of the clientele started calling me a "bitch" and a "whore" and several people at one table were watching poo porn and hooting very loudly. They seemed to love their meal, and yet they lingered at their table for hours afterwards, criticizing the owner and the food?

When I mentioned to the waiter,"The fries are a bit greasy," immediately a person at the next table leaned over and started screaming at me, saying, "You stupid c#$%t, how dare you criticize anything? Don't claim you know how to eat!"

I would love to come back, but really, some of the people who eat here are shit.

People thought your review was: Useful 2, Funny 1, Cool 2

I joined the world of gaming as a little girl. It was where I first discovered my voice and felt accepted. I found a community through the Ultima Dragons that I didn't have anywhere else in my life. During all that time I spent online I was never shamed for my enthusiasms. Never made to feel that I didn't deserve to be heard because of my gender. And I wouldn't be who I am without that community.

It's hard for me to imagine how that same fourteen-year-old girl might find a place to belong in the gaming world that exists today, with strong voices pushing her back, harassing her, questioning her authenticity with the unspoken threat: *Fit in the way we want you to or get out.* I don't know if I could handle that kind of environment. Perhaps I would hide my gender. Or just quit games entirely.

But I don't think those choices are acceptable for anyone. So if my speaking up made one person feel like they belong or prevented one person from stifling their own voice, then it was absolutely worth it.

Because if you can't be your own weird self on the internet, where can you be? And what would be the point?

It's Been Real

Let's wrap this up with some peppy
"Go, internet!" thoughts!

In January of 2014, an executive from YouTube took me and my business partner to lunch to inform us that the company wouldn't be investing in Geek & Sundry or any of the other original content channels anymore. The two-year funding experiment was over. We were on our own.

I left the restaurant, got in my car, and drove exactly one block. Then I pulled over and burst into tears.

Of joy.

No, it wasn't PMS. (Maybe.) It was relief that I could be free to follow my own compass again. Concentrate more on less. And maybe have a digital vacation and log offline for a bit? (Psh, don't get crazy, girl.)

I immediately went home and wrote down the top things I'd learned going from naïve actress to inexperienced web series show runner to world-weary start-up lady with Geek & Sundry.

- Find out where you are weakest.
Plug those holes up w/ the best
person you can find. Then let
them do their thing.
- Sign on to the daily work, not
the payoff.
- Dont let the world run you.
Run IT.
- The more mistakes, the better
the story afterwards.
Especially if there's a happy
ending.

I learned everything about creating and businessing the "stab me in the eye" way, but wow, did it feel good to take a moment to realize how much I'd grown over the past five years. And eventually, it led me down the best path I could ever have imagined.

In July 2014, I sold my company to Legendary Entertainment. The coolest, nerdiest company in Hollywood. After a lot of meetings, it was clear: HERE was a partner who would be fun to hang out with at Comic-Con.

The head of the company, Thomas Tull, isn't a Hollywood dude, he's a MATH GUY. We had a conversation about fluid dynamics and comic books the first time we met and I thought, *Wow, this guy is the coolest CEO bigwig I've ever met. I haven't met many, but he's definitely the coolest.*

Today I work with my company to create and produce shows for the web and television, write things like this book, act in tons of interesting projects, and still tweet and do conventions and stay connected with people in my online community every day. I've carved out the perfect job for myself, and the world has opened up to me in a way that I could never have imagined as a weird homeschooled kid writing in that little pink diary.

. . .

A few years ago I took a trip to George Lucas's Skywalker Ranch. (One of the employees was a big *Guild* and *Dr. Horrible* fan, so we got a private tour. I take advantage of stuff like that, because, uh, why not?) We toured a huge warehouse filled with props and wardrobe pieces from *Star Wars* and *Indiana Jones.* I hover-touched the REAL DEATH STAR.

VERY RARELY....

I AM A BALLER

Yeah, it was amazing. You can touch me and secondhand hover-touch the real Death Star, too. (Use some hand sanitizer first, please.)

At one point I stopped at a shelf with some odd-looking grenade objects, colorful but rough around the edges.

"What are these?"

"Oh, they're from *Star Wars*. Part of the power generator inside the shield generator on Endor."

I looked closer. "They look . . . janky. What are they made out of?"

"Dixie Cups."

"Wait, what? You mean the . . ."

"Yes, the disposable cups. They're spray-painted, see?" My guide lifted up the prop delicately and turned it over for me. Sure enough, I could see that underneath all the paint and decoration was a cup I could pull from a dispenser next to an office water bottle.

"Um . . . what?"

"During the filming of *Star Wars*, Lucas ran out of money, and the studio wouldn't give him more. He invested his own money in the film in exchange for the merchandising rights . . ."

". . . and that's why he's a billionaire."

"Right. But they still had to cut a lot of corners. Some of the props, even wardrobe pieces like the cuffs on the slave Leia costume, had to be cobbled together any way they could."

"By painting Dixie Cups." I stared at the prop in awe. It probably cost half a penny to make, and was a piece of the biggest movie franchise ever created. Definitely the most inspiring object I'd ever seen.

Now, I know bringing George Lucas into the mix might be setting the bar a WEE bit high, but the point is that he believed in his vision enough to make it happen NO MATTER WHAT. No one in the movie business wanted to make sci-fi movies at the time. The genre was completely disdained. Lucas believed in himself enough to put in his own money and use whatever resources he had to make his movie happen. And he found out, "Hey, billions of people feel the same way I do about sci-fi movies!"

With the help of frickin' Dixie Cups.

That same motto "I am determined to create something or express myself, no matter how hard it is, even if my mom is the only one who sees it!" is the embodiment of how I view the web. For the first time, everyone has a chance to have his or her voice heard, or to create a community around something they're passionate about and connect with other people who share that passion. Best of all, it rewards people and ideas that never would have made it through the system and allows the unique and weird to flourish.

I love the idea of breaking the system. And the beauty of the internet is that it gives everyone, especially unrepresented voices, the opportunity to do a little breaking. (Perot, I just can't quit you!)

It might be extremely dorky to point out, but who you are is singular. It's science. No one else in existence has your point of view or exact genome (identical twins and clones, look for inspiration elsewhere, please). That is why we need people to share and help us understand one another better. And on a bigger level than just taking a selfie. (Not hating on selfies, but a few is enough. You look good from that angle; we get it.) We need the world to hear more opinions, give glimpses into more diverse subcultures. Are you REALLY into dressing your cat in handcrafted, historically authentic outfits? No problem, there are people out there who want to see that! Probably in excruciating detail!

I was raised incredibly weird, but one day I accidentally got brave and thought I had a unique point of view about gaming. I decided to jump into web video—a world I knew very little about—to express it. Who knew there was anyone out there who wanted to listen?

I believe the next Oprah Winfrey or George Lucas will not come from a local news desk or college film program. He or she will come from the world of the web. Where the bar to entry is low, and where a group of kids can dream up a story and shoot it in their backyards. Regardless of whether someone gave them permission or not.

I hope all my copious oversharing encourages someone to stop, drop, and do something that's always scared them. Create something they've always dreamt of. Connect with people they never thought they'd know. Because there's no better time in history to do it.

So bust through all the cat GIFs and top-ten linkbait and share something of yourself. If you enrich one other person's life, it will be worth it. If you find one friend, it will be worth it.

Plus, the apocalypse may be right around the corner. And then there's that global warming thing happening.

I hope people will realize by the next century that global warming isn't a joke but by then the earth will of been destroyed by a meteor, a war, spinning out of orbit, the sun dying, all animal & plant life become extinct or the race will die out. well at that cheery note I leave you, Love LD

So take advantage of this time like it's a 2-for-1 sale, baby!
Good talk.
OXXO
Felicia

Thanks, Guys!

To my brother, Ryon, who made me laugh while writing when I'd IM him with questions and have conversations like this one:

Felicia Day

WHAT ARE YOU DOING?!

Felicia Day

Hey do you remember when we were driving to Florida and Grandma pulled a Taser on Mom and then Mom threatened to leave her on the side of the road?

Tuesday, January 7, 2014 8:57 PM

Ryon Day

yeah I remember that one!

ha ha it is to laff

that was the trip the dog died on and we weren't there!

Wednesday, January 8, 2014 9:23 AM

Felicia Day

Oh I didn't remember the dog died during that trip! Thanks, good detail!

Wednesday, January 8, 2014 9:24 AM

That story didn't make it in the book, but reliving our childhoods made us laugh together. For his help in delving into our past dysfunctions, I give the biggest thanks to him.

To my aunt Kate, who taught me the joy of pretend.

To my dad, because he's always made me feel like a success, no matter what I've done. And who will ALWAYS bug me to keep saving more in my retirement fund.

To my boyfriend, who kept me going through a lot of the crap I just threw up on all the previous pages. I'd delete my Twitter account for you, honey.

To Kim Evey, who was my companion and inspiration through the best and worst. Without you, this book wouldn't exist.

To Wil Wheaton, Sean Becker, Ryan Copple, Maurissa Tancheroen, and the cast of *The Guild* and *Dr. Horrible*, all of whom fuel my creativity and inspire me to be a better friend.

To Joss Whedon, whom I adore with stars in my eyes, who I want to be a badass for. Who inspires me to keep creating while standing awkwardly near the hummus.

To my agent, Erin, and my editor, Lauren, and everyone at Touchstone who believed that people wanted to hear stories from the life of a very weird internet woman.

And lastly, to every fan who's linked or tweeted or commented on my work. To every person who ever worked on or volunteered on *The Guild*. You kept me going. You turned my struggle into a success. You are the only reason I'm here. Love you muchly.

About the Author

Felicia Day is a professional actress who has appeared in numerous mainstream television shows and films, including a two-season arc on the Syfy series *Eureka* and a four-season arc on the CW show *Supernatural*.

However, Day is best known for her work in the web video world, behind and in front of the camera. She costarred in Joss Whedon's Emmy Award–winning internet musical *Dr. Horrible's Sing-Along Blog*. She also created and starred in the hit web series *The Guild*, which ran for six seasons and is currently available for viewing on every major digital outlet, including Netflix.

In 2012, she launched a YouTube channel called Geek & Sundry. The network has garnered more than 1.3 million subscribers to date and more than 200 million views. In 2014, the company was purchased by Legendary Entertainment. Day continues to act as CCO and develop web content and television projects with Legendary as a producer, writer, and performer. She is also extremely active on social media, has over 2.4 million Twitter followers, and is the eighth most followed person on Goodreads, where she is also the founder of Vaginal Fantasy, a romance and fantasy book club with more than 13,000 members.